Thomas Lewis O'Beirne

A short History of the last Session of Parliament

Thomas Lewis O'Beirne

A short History of the last Session of Parliament

ISBN/EAN: 9783337106997

Printed in Europe, USA, Canada, Australia, Japan

Cover: Foto ©ninafisch / pixelio.de

More available books at **www.hansebooks.com**

A SHORT

HISTORY

OF THE

LAST SESSION

OF

PARLIAMENT,

WITH

REMARKS.

O'Beirne, Thomas Lewis

—— ET CRIMINE AB UNO
DISCE OMNES. VIRG.

LONDON:

PRINTED FOR J. ALMON, AND J. DEBRETT, OPPOSITE
BURLINGTON HOUSE, PICCADILLY.

M DCC LXXX.

A SHORT

HISTORY, &c.

THE Period is arrived to which the nation has long looked forward with the greateſt anxiety, and earneſtneſs of expectation. The truſt veſted in their Repreſentatives by the People, is again returned to themſelves. They are empowered by the Conſtitution to require an account of their ſtewardſhip from thoſe to whom they had committed the care of their moſt important intereſts; and either to confirm them in that truſt in approbation and reward of their fidelity, or to puniſh the iniquity that has abuſed their confidence, by transferring it to others.

In the People thus determining for themſelves in their collective capacity, the thinking part of the nation has of late placed their only hopes of deliverance, from our preſent ſtate of domeſtic and foreign ignominy.

Tha

That all the calamities entailed upon this country, owe their origin and progrefs to the Corruption of Parliament, is a fact that will hardly be controverted. Without that blind and implicit obedience, which the Majority of the Commons have indifcriminately paid to every Adminiftration, under every fhifting of Government, through every change and fluctuation of contradictory meafures for fo many years paft, the nation could never have fallen a facrifice, as it has done, to the ignorance, incapacity and folly, of the moft profligate fet of men, that ever entailed ruin on the nation they governed.

As the corruption of Parliament, therefore, has been the fource of our calamities, the redrefs of them can only be expected from its reftoration to Freedom and Independency. However hopelefs the attempt was, of obtaining fo defirable a bleffing from their own voluntary repentance and atonement, yet it has been made. It was at the time, the only expedient the Conftitution fuggefted. The event is too well known. To their breach of truft, they added mockery and infult. Their treachery to their Conftituents, they aggravated by an avowal of their crime, that ended in an accumulation of paft injuries. They confeffed that they had fold themfelves to the purpofes of the Crown; that they had joined with its fervants in heaping on their country the evils of which it complained; yet, at the fame inftant

ftant of time, they perfifted, in conjunction
with thofe fervants, to withhold every hope
of redrefs; thus throwing afide even the appearance of fhame and decency, and feeming
to make a boaft of their having plunged
themfelves into the laft fink of proftitu-
tion.

What then was left for us, but to wait
for the prefent Period, when the power they
had fo wantonly abufed, fhould be taken
from them; when the People fhould have
their redrefs in their own hands, and an
opportunity would be given them of affert-
ing their own rights, and fulfilling the
wifhes and hopes of all good men.

To doubt of their difpofition to fulfill
thofe hopes, or to confound the national
character in the fame invective that branded
the corruption of Minifters, and the degeneracy of Parliament, has been refented by
fome as little lefs than treafon againft the
State. The fpirit that broke forth in the
late county affemblies, was maintained to
encourage this prejudice in favour of public virtue. It grounded a conclufion, that
whenever the appeal fhould be carried to the
Freeholders at large, in a manner clearly
and unequivocally provided by the Conftitution, they would be found as true to their
interefts, and as incorruptibly tenacious of
their rights as the moft virtuous and independant of their anceftors.

I will not enter on the difcuffion of this
queftion. Taken merely as matter of argument,

ment, it would, at beſt, be uſeleſs. All occaſion of controverſy will ſoon be ſuperſeded
by proof. The immediate deciſion is in the
hands of thoſe whoſe diſpoſitions and principles would give matter to the diſpute.

I can only aſſure them, that this nation
never knew a more important or momen-
tous criſis than the preſent; or one, that,
on their parts, called for ſo much vigilance,
caution and integrity. I will even venture
to affirm, that on their deciſion, the Liberties of this country, and all her future hap-
pineſs or miſery, abſolutely and finally de-
pend. I will lay it down as a prophetic
truth, which derives none of its forebode-
ings from viſionary fears, or unwarranted
apprehenſions, that if by their ſuffrages,
they return to the next Parliament a majority of thoſe men, who for the laſt ſix years,
have held themſelves independent of their
Conſtituents, and acted as the repreſentatives of the Miniſter, and not of the People, they will ſet the laſt ſeal to their own
ſlavery. They will irrevocably fix the period of their departed Liberties; they will
eſtabliſh the commencement of that æra
that ſees them reduced to the ſame degenerate ſtate with ſo many neighbouring nations, who were once as free as we have
been.

A long and hopeleſs independence of
ſeven years, is to ſucceed. Fearleſs of their
reſentment, and as regardleſs of their future, as they have been of their paſt complaints

plaints, their Reprefentatives will purfue their venal courfe, without fear or controul. And whoever attentively confiders the ftage from which they are to fet out, and fuppofes a progrefs in their proceedings proportionate to the changes that have taken place for the laft fix years, as well in point of national profperity, as in the temper and difpofitions of the People, will find, abundant reafon to admit my worft fears, and to form with me the moft gloomy apprehenfions.

If fuccefsful in the prefent ftruggle, the authors of thofe changes will have reafon to hold themfelves fupported by the People. They will not fail to perfevere in a fyftem, for which they can fo plaufibly plead the general approbation. They will maintain that the appeal has been made to the nation at large, and that the majority of the Freeholders hold the fame opinions with the majority of the Reprefentatives. That the degeneracy of Parliament was, as it always muft be, fympathetic, and the neceffary confequence of the degeneracy of the nation; and that by perfevering in their attempt to introduce the fyftem of government they have been fo long meditating, they only conform themfelves to the circumftances of the times, and the difpofitions of the People.

I beg, however, it may be underftood that I only moot the cafe, and that my fears are merely fuppofed. I am myfelf inclined to hope better things from the collected

virtue

virtue and integrity of the nation. It is not poffible that they can fo foon confent to forfeit the privileges their anceftors bled to preferve to them. They cannot fo tamely confent to relinquifh a Conftitution, the happy fruits of which they themfelves once enjoyed in the becoming pride of national glory, in the enjoyment of a free and un-interrupted commerce to every part of the globe, to moft of it exclufively, and in the increafe and fecurity of private property and domeftic happinefs.

My only wifh is to imprefs the People with a thorough fenfe of the great and de-cifive points on which the friends of this country, and the friends of the Miniftry, are actually at iffue before them. The pains that will be taken by both parties to influence their votes, will be in proportion to the vaft and important confequences that muft follow their determination.

But in this conteft, the advantages on both fides are by no means equal. On the part of the Minifter will be the weight and authority of government, and that all-rul-ing influence of the Crown, to which all our fufferings are afcribable, the numberlefs tribe of Placemen, Penfioners, and Retain-ers of Officers, difperfed through every corner and cranny of the Kingdom, and above all, the command of the public trea-fures, and all the fources of bribery and corruption—fources by which he has al-ready bought up the virtue and integrity of Parliament, and by which he depends

to

to be equally fuccefsful among their Conftituents.

By this laft expedient, he will be enabled
to employ his agents in the moft barbarous
and infulting tyranny that ever a deluded
People fubmitted to. He will make them the
fellers at once and the purchafers of their
own freedom and property. The treafures,
which he has levied on their indigence by
every oppreffive mode of taxation, under pretence of the exigencies of the State, he will
lavifh in buying from the voters the return
of thofe very men, who affifted him in
creating thofe exigencies, and whofe intereft
it is, as well as his own, that they fhould
increafe inftead of leffening.

To thefe corrupt auxiliaries will be added
all the arts of falfhood and mifreprefenta-
tion, and the fame caufes I have enumerated
above will give thefe alfo circulation and
fuccefs. The fame calumnies, the fame illiberal invectives, the fame imputed crimi-
nality of motives, with which their hireling
writers have been accuftomed to brand their
opponents, will now be propagated with
increafed induftry. No pains will be neglected, no expences fpared from the Treafury, to lead the People into the moft fatal
of all errors, that of miftaking their friends
for their worft enemies, their worft enemies
for their friends.

Againft thofe dangerous and powerful
engines the friends of the People can only

C   oppofe

oppofe the importance of their caufe, the integrity of their intentions in the profecution of that caufe, and their zeal to avert the dangers that hang over their country. To the falfhoods and mifreprefentations of Government, they can only fet in contraft a plain and candid ftate of facts, on which the People may judge for themfelves. To offer thefe is all they can do. If the People are not true to themfelves in forming their judgment, and acting in confequence, it is not in the power of any fet of men, however zealous and well intentioned, to fave them.

To promote fo defireable a work is the intention of the following Effay. The Author is of opinion, that nothing can be better calculated to give a proper idea of the refpective merits of the parties, who now claim the confidence of the people, than a faithful narrative of the proceedings of the laft Parliament, impartially fubmitted to public confideration.

It is not my intention, however, to follow the Minifter and his adherents through the vaft variety of matter that has occurred within thefe laft fix years. This, in fact, would be no lefs than to write a complete hiftory of the decline of the moft powerful and formidable empire that ever was raifed by the virtue and induftry of a brave people.

Other States have verged to their fall by gradual and flow degrees. Their foundations

tions have been undermined by progreſſive evils, almoſt imperceptible at the time of their influence, and which the induſtry of ſubſequent hiſtorians was obliged to draw out in a regular ſeries, before they could trace them to their ſources.

But in the ſhort ſpace of little more than five years, the men, whom God in his wrath permitted to govern this country, aſſiſted and countenanced by the guardians of the people, have crouded all the calamities and diſaſters that have oppreſſed other nations in as many ages.

Shortly after the commencement of the preſent reign, Great Britain poſſeſſed the largeſt extent of territory, the greateſt ſhare of power and opulence, and, in all human foreſight, the moſt permanent ſtate of ſecurity and ſtability of any nation upon the earth. Reputation abroad, and concord at home, diſtinguiſhed that period as the moſt ſplendid and happy this Kingdom had ever known.

Every part of the empire and its dependencies enjoyed a ſtate of perfect tranquility. Our flag flew triumphant and unrivalled from one end of the globe to the other. The houſe of Bourbon was completely humbled. The family compact, if not really, was at leaſt effectually diſſolved. Their finances reduced, and their power, both by land and ſea, almoſt annihilated, they could not attempt to carry its objects

into

into execution, without expofing themfelves
to a renewal of all the miferies and difgraces
it had drawn after it on its firft formation.
Our Colonies had attained the full vigour
of manhood. They confidered themfelves
as bound to us by the indiffoluble ties of
common origin, common names, common
language, religion, *intereft*, and there fub-
fifted, between us and them, the happieft
reciprocation of wealth, affection, and
power.

The fcene indeed began foon to be re-
verfed. A fatal change was fhortly introduced into the fyftem of Government, and
good men began to form the moft melancholy forebodings of impending evils.

But it was referved to the days of the laft
Parliament, to adopt the fatal meafure that
has, in fo fhort a time, effected what it was
impoffible for the moft apprehenfive and ti-
morous minds to forecaft to their fears.

In 1775, the Nation was plunged into
the American war. From that accurfed
meafure, as from the womb of the Trojan
horfe, have iffued all our calamities. The
eye turns with horror from the difaftrous
catalogue. But they prefs upon our feelings with too importunate a weight to al-
low our oppreffed fpirits even a momentary
refpite—we can no more fly from them
than from a tainted and deadly atmofphere
that wraps and envelopes us wherever we
turn our fteps.

Abroad

Abroad—the Empire difmembered. Its former ftrength converted into its weaknefs. —Our Colonies revolted, and forming the bond of union to one of the moft danger-ous confederacies that ever confpired againft the Crown and People of Great Britain *— Abandoned by all our former friends and allies : even thofe of them, who are indebt-ed to us almoft for their exiftence, driven by the weaknefs and fottifhnefs of our Councils, with which they would think it a difgrace to conneƈt themfelves, into an arm-ed league, for the exprefs purpofe of fup-plying our enemies, and of co-operating with them in the long-wifhed for opportu-nity of overthrowing and annihilating our naval power.

At home, an impoverifhed people, op-preffed with accumulating taxes, (to which there is no profpeƈt of either meafure or end) ; diftraƈted councils ; faƈtions in the Cabinet, in Parliament, in the Navy, in the Army ; lofs of all credit and mutual confidence ; diminifhed rents, lands funk at leaft one-third in value ; daily bankruptcies ; difcontents breaking out into public aƈts of fedition and lawlefs violence ; the blood of citizens flowing through our ftreets in pu-nifhment of mifguided exceffes, to which the weaknefs and pufillanimity of Govern-ment had given rife ; the Kingdom abfo-lutely under the difcretion and power of a

---

* See the King's Speech, Nov. 1779.

military

military force, independant of the Civil Magiftrate *; an univerfal face of diftruft and difmay, and fearful expectation of fome decifive calamity, for which, in the confef- fion of all parties, our actual fituation fhould induce us to prepare our minds.

Thefe are facts of equal fhame, grief, and notoriety. There is not an individual who does not feel their truth in the utmoft extent of their moft baneful confequences; and it would be an infult on the common fenfe of the nation, to fuppofe that they ftood in need of any exhortation to refcue itfelf from the treachery of a fet of men, who co- operated with a weak and profligate Admini- ftration, in tumbling it from the height of glory and affluance, into fuch a gulph of mi- fery, poverty, difgrace, and almoft final ruin.

To enter into a detail of all the blunders on the part of Miniftry, and the fervile in- difcriminate compliance on the part of the Commons, that has reduced us to this me- lancholy fituation, would, as I have ob- ferved, be impoffible from the urgency of the prefent moment. I fhall therefore, con- fine myfelf to a brief narrative of the pro-

---

* At the time of the late riots in London, an order was iffued out for the Military to act, without waiting for the authority of the Civil Magiftrate. The violence of the rioters, and the remiffnefs of the magiftrates, ren- dered fuch an extraordinary ftretch of the prerogative neceffary. But Minifters greedily feized this opportu- nity, and extended the orders to every part of the king- dom, though fuch neceffity exifted in the capital alone. Thofe orders have not as yet been formally recalled.

ceedings of the last session. Most of the great events, that mark its features, will come home to the feelings of the People. They belong to their cognizance in a very peculiar manner, as immediately relating to the most declared and acknowledged duty they had a right to command from their Constituents. They alone are sufficient to answer all the salutary purposes which this essay is designed to produce.

But before I enter on the subject, it may not be amiss previously to state the situation of things, when the sixth session of the last Parliament was opened by a speech from the throne. The conduct of the majority of the Commons will thereby be more clearly illucidated, and their merits more fully understood by the People.

The disgraceful campaign of 1779, had just closed, and men had time to collect their thoughts, and to review the dangers they could scarce believe they had escaped. The combined fleets of France and Spain, the junction of which Ministers had not taken a single step to prevent, had retired into port, after having swept the channel in triumph for several weeks, and spread terror and dismay along our coasts. A strong easterly wind and an epidemic disorder, that desolated the crew of every ship in their squadron, had rescued us from their menaces, and frustrated their intended scheme of invasion. To these providential circumstances alone, it was acknowledged by all parties,

parties, we were indebted for our preserva-
tion. The enemy found the whole extent
of our coaft unarmed and unprovided. Ply-
mouth, to which they directed their firft attempts, was naked, defencelefs, and un-
covered. The fleet of England had been
ignominioufly chaced up the channel, and
compelled to take fhelter in its own har-
bours *. Squadrons of privateers infefted
every part of the coafts of the three kingdoms. They fpread terror through all the
maritime towns, and captured our mer-
chant fhips, even in fight of the fhore. All
trade was at a ftand. Our manufactures
were equally affected, and the lower orders
of the People crouded the ftreets idle and
unemployed. The merchants would not
venture to fhip off their goods, while the
channel was filled with the cruizers of
France, Spain, and America. The traders
and dealers of the maritime counties were
fearful of fending the commodities they
purchafed of the farmers, by fea, and were
thereby prevented from circulating them,
as they were accuftomed to do, by the cheap
conveyance of water-carriage. Thofe who
did run the rifque, did it under the difad-
vantage of an unheard-of infurance. This

---

* The fquadron under Sir Charles Hardy, remained
at Spithead, till the retreat of the enemy. It was then
ordered to put to fea, at the rifque of being difperfed
and fcattered by the ftorms that prevail at that feafon,
and this to anfwer no purpofe, but the purpofe of an
empty parade, and to amufe and delude the public.

afforded

afforded the freighters a pretext of buying them up at the loweſt rates, while at the ſame time it raiſed the markets to which they were ſent, as it was paid back by the purchaſer in the increaſed prices they coſt him. The conſequence was a failure of rent among the farmers, bankruptcies among the lower tradeſmen and artiſans, an univerſal diſtruſt and loſs of credit. The diſtreſſes into which thoſe evils natu-rally reduced the landed gentlemen, joined to a monopoly of money, by thoſe who ne-gociated the loans for government, reduced the value of lands from thirty-five and forty, to twenty-five, and twenty years pur-chaſe *.

Our accounts from abroad were all of the ſame diſaſtrous tenor. The Portugal trade remained locked out the whole ſummer. The Mediterranean and Levant trades were utterly gone. The Newfoundland fiſhery was nearly demoliſhed. The Eaſt India trade had taken refuge up the Shannon as far as Limerick. There it remained for ten weeks in conſtant terror, till being reſcued at length by the voluntary retreat of the enemy, it got into port, with the loſs of one fourth of the ſquadron, wrecked near the Iſle of Guernſey.

Our Weſt-India merchantmen had, in-deed, arrived in ſafety; but ſo unexpect-edly, and in a manner ſo contrary to all

* In one of the beſt counties in England, an eſtate was ſold laſt year for eighteen years purchaſe.

D human

human calculation, that Minifters themfelves were compelled to attribute the event
to the goodnefs of Providence alone.

From the Weft-Indies, every day brought
over the news of fome frefh difafter. Do-
minica captured—St. Vincent wrefted from
us—and Grenada once more reduced to the
dominion of France. If St. Lucia avoided
the fame fate, it owed its fafety to the gal-
lantry of Colonel Meadows *, and to the
fkill and intrepidity of Admiral Barrington,
who, with four men of war and a few fri-
gates, was left, *in this fecond year of hoftilities with France*, expofed to fourteen fail of
the line, under Monfieur D'Eftaign.

In America, that grave of Englifh valour
and of Englifh glory, things wore, if poffible, a ftill more unfavourable afpect.—
Rhode Ifland had been evacuated, and this
only fafe retreat † for our men of war, from
Halifax

---

* This gallant officer, who has been foremoft in
every action fince the beginning of the American war,
is ftill a lieutenant-colonel on the Englifh eftablifhment,
while half-pay lieutenants, and clerks in office, are at
the head of regiments.

† New-York is by no means a fafe harbour to make.
Exclufive of the fhallownefs of the bar, on which, with
fmooth water, and gentle winds, fixty four gun fhips
have often ftruck, there are very few points of the com-
pafs from which large fhips can run for it in a ftorm.
The North-weft, which are the prevailing high winds,
blow directly out of the bay; and fuppofing a large fleet
to be furprized by a gale from the South-eaft, a good
way within the large bay that is formed by the Eaft end
of Long Ifland, and the Capes of the Delaware, without daring to attempt the bar at Sandy-Hook, it would
be

Halifax to the Weſt-Indies, relinquiſhed
to the enemy, whóſe fleets are now riding
there, unoppoſed, and meditating hoſtilities
againſt our devoted army. All active, of-
fenſive operations were ſuſpended. The
whole attention of the immenſe force collected at New-York was taken up in pre-
paring for its defence, and guarding itſelf
from being ſurpriſed by an army, which
this infatuated country was made to believe
did not amount to five thouſand men.

Ireland was in a ſtate little ſhort of rebellion. Adminiſtration continued to turn
a deaf ear to her reiterated complaints, in
breach of the public faith pledged to her
the former ſeſſions; and her aſſociated corps
were then determined to extort, by force,
the redreſs ſhe had ſolicited in vain as a
mark of favour.

The very Miniſters were quarrelling a-
mong themſelves; and as it generally hap-
pens in ſuch caſes, their iniquitous ſecrets
had been divulged by ſome of their own
body. Lord Gower, who had acted with
them moſt ſteadily, and with the moſt forward zeal, and who had ſupported them
through ſo many dirty meaſures, had, *a few*

be ſcarce poſſible for them to avoid the ſhoals of Barne-
gat. Not one of theſe difficulties can be applied to
Rhode Iſland. The whole navy of England might get
in there with any wind, and ride there in ſafety. Yet
the nation is told that it has cauſe to triumph, becauſe
we have relinquiſhed that place to get poſſeſſion of
Charles Town, which a frigate cannot approach with
ſafety.

days

days before, relinquished his feat at the Council Board. The habitual indolence and inattention of the Minister, and his criminal neglect, which, he asserted, it was impossible to find words to exprefs, were the reasons he assigned for his resignation. Thefe he further strengthened by a public declaration from his feat in Parliament, that he could no longer act with such men with honour or conscience. To concur in their measures would be infamy, and a crime against his country, too much even for him to submit to *.

I beg of my readers that they would carefully attend to this detail of facts, and especially to the last circumstance. I have already given my reasons for thus particularly enumerating them. The Reprefentatives of the People, who at such a moment, and after such a declaration from the very Prefident of the King's councils, could continue to vote with the authors of thefe complicated calamities, and to give them a blind and implicit unenquiring support, can surely have little hopes of escaping the execration of their Constituents at this time of general account.

---

* This Nobleman was one the moft forward and fanguine among the Miniftry for enforcing hoftile meafures againft the Colonies. He has lived to fee his error, and, as far as a public acknowledgment goes, has made atonement to his country; yet a majority of the Reprefentatives of the People continued to fupport an obftinate perfeverance in that reprobated meafure.

Such,

Such, however, was the perilous situation of our affairs both abroad and at home when the Minister presumed to meet the Parliament. The defection of his colleagues, the loud cries of the public, the consciousness of his own inadequacy to the place, the conviction he must have felt that all the miseries of his country were solely to be ascribed to the ignorance and imbecility of his councils, seemed to have no weight with him. Secure in the numbers of his venal supporters in both Houses, which he had previously calculated, he equally set at defiance the clamours of the people, and the inquisitive indignation of the virtuous and patriotic within doors.

The immortal Pitt, in all the pride of his most brilliant successes, never met the great Council of the Nation, to congratulate with them on their victories, with more confidence than this man assumed, with such a load of national censure, and national calamity on his head.

The ADDRESS.

The Address, which he had the audacity to get proposed in the Upper House, set out with calling on the Peers to express their *conviction* of the *blessings* we enjoyed under his Administration. Let the reader but recollect the time, the circumstances, such as I have just described them; and then form
a judg-

a judgment of thofe Lords, who, through the perfon of their Sovereign, voted thanks to the Minifter for procuring *fuch bleffings* to the Nation.

The remainder of the addrefs was pretty much the fame in both Houfes. It was, as ufual, an echo to the fpeech, an eulogy on Adminiftration, and an unbounded promife on the part of the Commons, to levy on their Conftituents whatever fupplies an avowed profecution of the fame ruinous meafures that had caufed our misfortunes, fhould call for.

It was to no purpofe that the gentlemen of the Oppofition, reminded the Reprefen-tatives of the People, of the facred duty they owed to their Conftituents. In vain they afked them if they confidered that the awful moment was approaching, when they fhould be called upon to give an account of their ftewardfhips. With what face could they appear before their Conftituents? Could they inform them for what purpofe they had pledged themfelves to levy additional taxes, on a People already groaning under a debt not much fhort of one hundred and fifty millions, and which when the unfunded debt, and the expenditure of the fucceeding year were added to it, would be little fhort of two hundred millions, requiring an annual intereft of eight millions and a half? What reafons would they affign for fupporting a fet of men, under whofe baneful aufpices, we were reduced to that extremity of dif-

trefs

trefs, which the fpeech acknowledged ?
Would they fay that they fupported them
becaufe the glaring abfurdities, the criminal omiffions, and fcandalous inconfiftencies of their Adminiftration, had raifed the
* *moft dangerous confederacy, that ever was
formed againft the Crown and People of Great
Britain*; becaufe notwithftanding the im-
menfe fums that had been voted to the different fervices, far beyond the utmoft extravagance of any previous time, they left
the kingdom fo unprovided and defencelefs,
that nothing + *but the intervention of Providence
could have fruftrated the defigns and attempts
of our enemies to invade it.* Would they fay
that they fupported them, becaufe their own
colleagues, fpeaking like men willing to
make fome atonement for their errors, and
beholding fuch things as were tranfacting
among them, declared, that they could no
longer be prefent at their councils with honour or confcience ? What would they tell
their Conftituents had become of the Ame-
ricon war ? Minifters had paffed it over in
the filence of death. Neither in the Speech,
nor in the arguments of thofe who were in-
ftructed to move the Addrefs, was there a
fingle word dropt upon the fubject. Were
we to fit down content with the lofs of
the many millions, and the rivers of blood
fhed by our brave countrymen, which it
had already coft the nation ? Or was it ftill

---

* Vide King's Speech.　　　+ Ibid.

to continue to drain away the ſtrength that ſhould be turned againſt our natural enemies? They could not inform them. The Miniſter had not condeſcended to take the leaſt notice of it.

What excuſe would they tell them, had the Miniſter himſelf alledged to the Houſe? By what palliatives did he cover his own crimes? "I have always acted to the beſt "of my underſtanding. If my meaſures "have failed, they can at leaſt plead the "merit of goodneſs in my deſigns, and in- "nocence in my intentions. The perils with "which we are ſurrounded are not the fault "of my Adminiſtration. They are owing "to the ingratitude of the powers confede- "rated againſt us. Am I to blame if the "Colonies be diſloyal; if France be ambi- "tious, and if Spain be a dupe? I wiſhed to "have prevented the junction of the French "and Spaniſh fleets. I knew it was the only "meaſure that, under any human agency, "could poſſibly ſave us from deſtruction. "But the French had the ſagacity to know "my wiſhes. While the fleet of England "remained at anchor at Torbay, Monſieur "D'Orvilliers ſlipped out from Breſt, and "ſailed to Cadiz."

Theſe were, in fact, the chief, nay the only arguments made uſe of by the Miniſter to repel the attacks of the oppoſite ſide of the Houſe. An unbluſhing avowal of his ignorance, his incapacity, his inactivity, was his only plea to favour. "*He acted to the*
beſt

beſt of bis underſtanding." His crime was
his defence, and it was remarked that he
urged it with ſuch inſolence as nothing but
the venality of Parliament could have in-
ſpired him with. He had previouſly taken
care to render his defence, whatever it
might be, unanſwerable. The majority of
the Members had ſacrificed, at the Treaſury, all the ſacred obligations they owed
to their Conſtituents.

It is worthy of being obſerved to the
Freeholders, on this occaſion, that during
the whole debate on the Addreſs, not one
Engliſhman opened his lips in approbation
of the Miniſter or his meaſures, except the
Secretary at War, and he only ſpoke in
anſwer to accuſations urged againſt himſelf.
Two Scotch advocates, one of them now a
Peer, and at the head of one of the Courts of
Law, and a Gentleman of the ſame country,
who in conſideration of ſome military pre-
ferments, which he has ſince received, was
that very day enrolled on the Treaſury liſt,
were the only perſons who openly ſtood up
for the firſt Miniſter of England, in the
Parliament of England, at a criſis when
meaſures that tended to her very exiſtence
were under deliberation. But, alas ! what
do I talk of deliberation. The Miniſter
ſcorned to aſk the advice of Parliament,
even at ſo perilous a criſis. The *form* of
the approbation of the Majority, to the meaſures he had already *determined* on, was all

E   he

he called for. They could not refufufe him
his own. He had bought it at a price *.

I R E L A N D.

Towards the clofe of the laft feffion, the
diftreffes of Ireland had become the fubject
of parliamentary attention. The 11th of
May, on a motion of the Marquis of Rock-
ingham, an unanimous addrefs was voted,
recommending to his Majefty's moft ferious
confideration, the diftreffed and impoverifhed
ftate of the loyal and well-deferving People
of that kingdom, and praying that fuch fteps
might be taken, as fhould tend to promote
the common ftrength, wealth, and commerce, of his Majefty's fubjects in both
kingdoms. The following day his Majefty
returned a gracious anfwer to this addrefs,
and promifed to give directions to comply
with the prayer of it. A confiderable time
elapfed however, and not a fingle ftep was
taken by Adminiftration in this important
and preffing bufinefs. The recefs was at
hand The clamours of the People of Ireland became more loud and vehement, in

* " A fullen Majority," faid one of the Country gentlemen, " filent within doors, loquacious without. In
" every other place, but in the Houfe, to the amaze-
" ment of all fpeculative politicians, condemning the
" meafures, and execrating the men whom they came
" there to fupport."—Would to God that fo fhameful
a record could be concealed from the knowledge of fo-
reigners, and the refearches of our defcendants.

propor-

proportion as their diftreffes increafed, and their hopes of redrefs appeared more remote. It was evident to the moft inattentive obferver, that fome effectual remedy fhould be immediately applied, or that the moft fatal confequences were to be apprehended from the defpair of a brave People, reduced to fuch a ftate of calamity and diftrefs, as was experienced by no other nation that ever exifted, unlefs fcourged by war, peftilence, or famine.

Upon this fhameful contempt of the recommendation of Parliament, and this breach of affurances folemnly pledged by the fervants of the Crown, a motion was made on the 2d of June, reftating the neceffity of giving fpeedy and effectual relief to Ireland, and intreating, that if the Royal Prerogative vefted in his Majefty, was not adequate to adminifter the neceffary relief, he would be pleafed to continue the Parliament of this kingdom, and give orders forthwith for calling the Parliament of Ireland. To induce the Minifter to concur in this motion, all the confequences that afterwards took place, were predicted and fet in the ftrongeft colours. He was told that he was already confidered by the People of Ireland, as having declared open hoftility againft their country. He had thrown out, by his fole influence, a trifling favour, which before his coming down, and oppofing it with all the energy of his eloquence, as well as authority, the Commons feemed difpofed to grant them. If to this he

E 2   would

would add a contempt of the united wifhes of
the Britifh Legiflature, and perfevere in refufing them relief, there was no forefeeing to
what fatal exceffes, their indignation and defpair might tranfport them. The example of
America, was fet before his eyes. He was ex-
horted not to drive this only furviving child
of Great Britain into fimlar circumftances,
or compel her to extort as a right, what fhe
wifhed to receive as a favour. But nothing
could rouze him from his obftinate inactivity.
He indulged his lethargic indolence in the
fecurity of his influence and numbers. The
Parliament of England was prorogued. No
orders were fent to convene the Parliament
of Ireland.

From this unfeeling inattention to the diftreffes of that kingdom, and this contempt
of its poffible and natural refentments, the
Minifter proceeded to a renunciation of its
Government. He refufed them protection
in the hour of their greateft danger, and
virtually releafed its inhabitants from their
allegiance.

Spain had acceded to the French and
American confederacy. Both channels were
overrun by the fleets of the Allies. Ireland,
as well as England, was threatened with invafion, and the enemy had actually begun
to infult her maritime towns. In this emer-
gency, fhe applied to Government for protection. But alas! the gallant troops that
could have avenged her caufe upon her in-
vaders, were wafting their ftrength in the

wilds

wilds of America, in the profecution of a cruel and favage war, againſt her fellow-fubjeċts. She received from the Miniſter, the anſwer that was returned to our anceſtors, on a fimilar application to the Senate of Rome; " You muſt arm in your own defence, we have not the power to protect you."

Thus was the Government abdicated, and the People abandoned to their fate. But they were not wanting to themſelves. They found in their national bravery and virtue defence, not only againſt the arms of their foreign enemies, but againſt the fatal effects and complicated evils of mal-adminiſtration at home; of calamity entailed upon them by tyranny without hopes of redreſs; of iron-handed power without protection. They exhibited a political phœnomenon. They transformed weakneſs into ſtrength. From the loweſt ebb of national miſery and public dependency they ſuddenly roſe into the fullneſs of vigour, ſpirit, and ability to command a redreſs of all their grievances.

Forty thouſand men, completely armed, regularly difciplined, felected from the nobility, gentry, merchants, citizens, and reſpectable yeomanry, clothed, furniſhed, and maintaned at their own expence, firſt fecured their country againſt its foreign enemies, and then united their efforts in *compelling* that juſtice with arms in their hands, that had, as with America, been denied to humble applications, and the repeated re-
preſen-

prefentations of their mifery and diftrefs.
They peremptorily infifted upon that redrefs which they had before fupplicated.—
Their demands were enforced by the points
of forty thoufand bayonets.

Yet amid this fcene of danger, while this
fpirit of refiftance looking towards independency, dictated the refolves of every meeting of the Affociators, and peremptorily
controuled the deliberations of the Great
Council of the kingdom, the Minifter, to
whofe fhameful inattention and criminal
neglect in the firft ftages of the difcontents,
it was folely imputable, ftill remained undecided and inactive. He confeffed that he
had never properly turned his thoughts to
the fubject. He was ignorant of the danger, and confequently was unprovided with
a remedy. He hefitated, protracted, fhuffled,
nor was it till the 13th of December that,
baited and goaded on by the importunate
attack of the friends of their country, he
came down to the Houfe, and directed his
creatures to acquiefce in whatever propofitions Ireland might think proper to demand. Whether thofe propofitions were
derogatory to the glory, or contrary to the
commercial interefts of this Kingdom ----
or whether they would throw too great a
weight into the fcale of Ireland, was then
no time to confider. There was no longer
any room for deliberation. Minifters had
let the moment pafs when the refpective
rights of the two countries might be delibe-
rately

rately adjufted, and when Ireland would have refted content with indulgencies far fhort of what fhe was fairly entitled to expect. The exigency of the moments, thanks to our wife and provident rulers, left no other alternative but an implicit acquiefcence or another civil war, and no facrifice could be thought too great that, in our prefent fituation, would prevent a diffolution of the conftitutional connexion between the two countries.

During the whole of this important bufinefs, the majority of the Reprefentatives of the People, as ufual, followed the Minifter through all his fhiftings and windings, contradictions and inconfiftencies. They watched over him in the flumbers of his indolence and inactivity—they ftood by him in his ftarts of peremptorinefs and obftinacy. They denied when he refufed; when he relaxed, they granted; they gave their fanction to his meafures before they were put into execution, and they fcreened him from cenfure when their baneful effects became notorious, and called not only for redrefs but punifhment.

It is impoffible to read the account of this important bufinefs without calling to mind the beginnings of the unfortunate conteft with America, and comparing the conduct of Minifters towards the two countries I find this done in fo mafterly a manner in the fubftance of Mr. Burke's Speech, on the 6th of December, publifhed in Almon's

mon's Debates, that I shall content myself
with transcribing it for the benefit of my
readers.

" Ireland spurned at the British claim
" of dominion ; she looked upon herself
" free and independent. A mob had rose
" in Dublin, and non-importation agree-
" ments had taken place. Why not, as
" was the fate of Boston, shut up the
" Port of Dublin? Why not burn Corke,
" reduce Waterford to ashes ?---Why not
" prohibit all popular meetings in that
" kingdom, and destroy all popular elec-
" tions ?---Why not alter the usual mode of
" striking juries, as was done by the Maf-
" fachufet's Bay Charter Bill ?---Why not
" bring the Dublin rioters over to this
" country to be tried by an English jury?
" Why not shut up their ports, and pre-
" vent them from trading with each other?
" Why not prescribe the principal lead-
" ers, who hold commissions, not under the
" Crown, but by virtue of the free elec-
" tion of the very corps which they com-
" manded ?—Why not put them out of
" the King's peace, and declare the whole
" Kingdom in rebellion ? The answer was
" plain and direct. Ministers dare not.—
" Sad and dear-bought experience had
" taught them the folly, as well as imprac-
" ticability of such measures. The danger
" of the present awful moment made in-
" solence and arrogance give way to fear
" and humiliation."

ARMY

ARMY ESTIMATES, &c.

In the midſt of the debates on this imminent danger, to which the nation was expoſed from an interior convulſion, ſimilar to what the fatal meaſures of Adminiſtration had raiſed in America, the buſineſs of the ſupplies was carried on as uſual. The majority of the Repreſentatives of the People, heedleſs of the diſtreſſes of their Conſtituents, were voting away their money without meaſure, account, or enquiry. To ſuch a height of inſolence and effrontery had their ſecurity in the venal ſupport of Parliament elated the Miniſters, that the Secretary at War openly aſſigned, as a ground for his application for the enormous land-force he meant to have paid, what amounted to an impeachment of the Firſt Lord of the Admiralty. That Miniſter had, from his ſeat in Parliament, confeſſed, that a perſon in the office he filled, who ſhould not always have in readineſs a fleet equal to the combined force of the houſe of Bourbon, deſerved to loſe his head. Yet his worthy colleague, Mr. Jenkinſon, did not heſitate to inform the Commons, that the neceſſity of augmenting the army aroſe from the alarming inferiority of our fleet *, and its conſequent inability to give that protection
and

---

* Here the Secretary at War aſſigns the *weak ſtate* of the navy, as the cauſe of the great ſupplies required for the army. Lord North, on opening his Budget, in-

F   formed

and fecurity, either to the Kingdom itfelf
or its dependencies abroad, which, in all
former wars, had been derived from that
eftablifhment. The forces to be employed
he ftated at 179,500 men; and for their
pay and cloathing, he demanded no lefs a
fum than 4,130,000 l.

A military eftablifhment, that fo infinite-
ly furpaffed whatever had been heard of before in this country, fpread a general alarm
among thofe gentlemen who had invariably
oppofed the fyftem that had reduced us to
a ftate, which called for fo enormous a
force. Not that they objected to raife the
required numbers. The exigencies of the
times, however created, might make the
meafure neceffary. But the Country Gentlemen, in particular, were loud in calling
on the Houfe to confider, before they gave
their votes, how far it was wife and politic
to agree to the eftimates; how far the re-
maining refources of this oppreffed and impoverifhed country, were adequate to the
fupport of the unparallelled expence, which
they would occafion.

As to the policy of agreeing to them, it
was urged, that it would be the utmoft ex-

formed the Houfe, that it was the *greatnefs of our navy
eftablifhment* that devoured the refources of the country,
and to that he principally attributed the enormity of the
laft year's expences. In fuch contempt do Minifters
hold the underftanding of Parliament! So heedlefs are
they of the language in which they addrefs them! Thus
do they all join in fporting with the fufferings of their
country!

travagance

travagance of political infanity, for this
country ever to rely on any other fecurity
or mode of defence, than that of a proper
naval force. A defence, which our infular
fituation, and the experience of all paft
times, pointed out to Great-Britain as her
natural fecurity. To confefs ourfelves weaker
on that element to which we owed all our
wealth, glory, and importance, as the Secretary at War had done, and to acknowledge with him that we were incapable of
remedying that weaknefs, by any other
means, than that of a land army, was the
moft alarming and afflicting intelligence,
that Parliament ever conveyed to the nation.

As to the inadequatenefs of the nation
to fupport the expence, if there were any
who were not blind to what ftared every
man (except thofe who wilfully fhut their
eyes) in the face, they might foon be convinced from the forcible teftimony of de-
creafed rents, ruined farms, and bankrupt
tenants. The deferted fields, the towns
empty of manufacturers, and fwarming
with foldiers, and the gaols crowded with
reduced tradefmen and farmers, would afford the moft melancholy and irrefragable
proofs of the general poverty and diftrefs.

But if the exigencies of the times compelled the Reprefentatives of the People, to
vote the eftimates as they ftood, they were
called upon at leaft, not to vote them pre-
cipitately, or without examination. Before
they gave away fo enormous a fum of the
money of their Conftituents, they fhould

at leaſt know to what objects ſuch a force would be directed; what uſe was to be made of it, or how far it was applicable and adequate to effect the great purpoſe of the war, the obtaining a ſpeedy and honourable peace. They ſhould be aſſured that the ſtricteſt œconomy ſhould be obſerved in the expenditure, and that no part of that ſum, or of the enormous extraordinaries and contingencies that would be tacked to it, ſhould be plundered from the Public by ruinous contracts, uſurious Jobs, and all the douceurs with which Miniſters purchaſed ſupport and influence, out of the public purſe.

Theſe, and ſuch like arguments, were preſſed upon the Houſe with all the warmth of zeal, and the energy of eloquence. But to the queſtions that were propoſed to the Miniſters to obtain the wanted information, they returned a ſullen ſilence; or if they were ſo cloſely preſſed as to be compelled to riſe, and ſay ſomething in their defence, they were not prepared;—they had not brought their papers;—they were not reſponſible.—Their creatures called for the queſtion, and the ſmall, though urgent voice of the Friends of the People, was drowned by the clamours of the Treaſury-Bench*.   MID-

* In the courſe of this debate, Mr. Townſhend called on the Secretary at War, to aſſign a reaſon why the expences of the ſtaff for the preſent year, ſhould be 82,000l. while the ſtaff of that glorious year 1762, was but 69,000l. He thought the Houſe had a right to aſk in
                                                                    the

MIDDLESEX ELECTION.

While the Truftees of the Public Purfe, were thus facrificing the interefts of their Conftituents to the favour of the Minifter within doors, he was himfelf no lefs active without, in attempting to violate the moft effential of their rights in the free choice of their Reprefentatives. On a vacancy for Middlefex, Mr. Byng, an independent Gentleman of the county, was called upon by the declared fenfe of the Freeholders, to offer himfelf a candidate in the room of their late Member. To comply with their defires, it was requifite that he fhould vacate the feat he already held in Parliament, and with this view he applied to the Minifter for the nominal place of the Chiltern Hundreds. On this application he received a letter from the Minifter, informing him that he had already *given a vacating feat* to a Member of Parliament who meant to offer himfelf for the County of Middlefex, and that he could not *give* another.

The Gentleman, to whom this preference was given, was Col. Tuffnel, Member for Beverley, and a creature of the Duke of Northumberland, Lord Lieutenant of the

the name of their Conftituents, on what grounds this excefs of 13,000l. fhould be voted. The anfwer received from the Secretary was, that he did come down prepared on the fubject, and therefore could not fatisfy the Houfe. The fame anfwer he repeated the next day, and there the matter has refted.

County.

County. It was known at the time, and the event has placed it beyond a doubt, that this candidate was brought forward in direct oppofition to the wifhes of the Freeholders. Yet by refufing to *give* a vacating feat, as this great arbiter of our privileges, exprefſed himſelf, to the object of their choice, the Minifter feemed determined to compel the Electors to accept him.

Here was an avowed and barefaced attack upon the Freedom of Election beyond the utmoft infolence of all former Minifters. It was no fecret intrigue managed in the dark, by concealed agents, and under-hand inftruments, but a direct, formal, open robbery, on the moft valuable franchife, the fubject can boaft. If the attempt had been crowned with fuccefs, we fhould not have had even a hope of fafety left. The precedent would have been eftablifhed. Adminiftration would have claimed a prefcriptive right of difcharging from the fervice of his Conftituents any member whom they might pleafe to favour, and of deciding who fhould offer themfelves to the Electors, for their choice.

But fortunately the attempt was made on a body of Freeholders, whofe independent fpirit has, on all occafions, fet an example to the Kingdom of the moft commendable zeal and activity in the prefervation of the firft and deareft of their rights. They fpurned at the combination that had been formed againft them, and as they could not have the candidate of their wifhes, they prevailed on a Gentleman of the moft approved

proved

proved worth and difintereftednefs to ftep
between them and the creature of the Minifter, and they returned him unanimoufly *.

As foon as Mr. Wood took poffeffion of
his undifputed feat, he preferred a petition
to Parliament, complaining of this injury
that had been offered to one of the moft
effential and undoubted rights of the People. This petition contained a direct and
formal charge againft the Minifter by name.
It accufed him of a wanton and arbitrary
abufe of powers, which, if not wholly
ufurped, had, in many inftances fimilar to
the prefent, been exercifed to the utter fubverfion of all free election. It was figned
by a long lift of the moft refpectable Freeholders. The greateft part had, indeed, refufed to fet their hands to it. They conceived it to be a ufelefs attempt to addrefs
themfelves to Parliament even on fo notorious and crying an invafion of their rights,
and the fubfequent conduct of the Houfe
juftified the imputation. They fcreened
the Minifter from cenfure; they refufed the
Freeholders redrefs.

---

* It appeared that the whole of this bufinefs was a
juggle between Col. Tuffnel and the Minifter. His
Lordfhip had never given him the Chiltern Hundreds,
nor had he ever vacated his feat for Beverley. In the
courfe of the debate it appeared, from the teftimony of
Mr. Byng, that a man, who had been condemned to death
for coining, had been refpited becaufe he promifed to
procure the Treafury fifteen votes, in cafe of a conteft,
while a poor woman, who was under fentence for the
fame crime was, for want of fuch intereft, burnt.

OECO-

Oeconomy in the Public Expenditure.

At the time that this queftion took up the attention of the friends of their country within doors, a new fcene was opening without that promifed to produce the happy Reformation, to which alone it is on all hands agreed, the Nation can be indebted for its fafety.

The daily accumulating diftreffes of the country began at length to open the eyes of the Public to the fcandalous profufion with which all our affairs were carried on, and the neceffity of a ftrict and parfimonious œconomy in every department of the State. It was evident that the evil fo frequently foretold, and fo anxioufly dreaded by the friends of the Conftitution, had unfortutunately happened in our days. We had only to read the Journals of the Houfe to be convinced that the Crown had acquired fuch an irrefiftable weight of pecuniary influence, as to buy up all Public Virtue, and to turn the Conftitution againft itfelf. Parliament feemed to meet for nothing elfe than to eftablifh grievances, and fanctify them into laws. They voted every meafure that was propofed to them, without a fhadow of information, or the moft diftant enquiry into their tendency; they engaged their country in wars, without once examining into their juftice or expediency; they lavifhed away the money of their Conftituents without meafure or account. The Court had but

to

to propofe, and thofe creatures of its power acknowledged no other duty but to approve and fupport. Freedom of Debate, was become a term of mockery. Reafon and argument, were held in equal contempt with Patriotifm and Public Virtue. Even facts of the greateft notoriety were voted not to exift, and grievances, the moft public and acknowledged, were proved to be bleffings, by the more than almighty fiat of a majority of votes.

In vain did a few independent members in both Houfes, attached to the Conftitution, endeavour to oppofe this torrent of Corruption. Obftruction feemed but to increafe its violence. The more ardent and fpirited were their attacks on Adminiftration, the more lavifhly did thefe difperfe the crown treafures in the purchafe of frefh mercenaries to fight their battles. What then remained for the People but to take their caufe into their own hands ? To examine by themfelves into the origin of their fufferings, to trace the national calamities to their real fources, and inftruct their Reprefentatives, in the forms allowed them by the Conftitution, to procure ample redrefs.

The zeal and indefatigable induftry of fome of the leaders of Oppofition, had greatly contributed to convince the People of the immediate neceffity of fuch interference. On the 7th of December, the Duke of Richmond moved the Lords to prefent an humble Addrefs to his Majefty, befeeching his Majefty to reflect on the manifold diftreffes and difficulties in which this country

G   is

is involved, too deeply felt to ftand in need of enumeration, and to reprefent that, a-midft the many and various matters that required reformation, and muft undergo correction before this country could rife fu-perior to its powerful enemies : the wafte of public treafure called for inftant remedy. Among the many inftances of increafing profufion that came out in the debate on this motion, were the following. The ex-pence of foreign embaffies, in the glorious reign of King William, was about 43,000l. in the prefent, they had fwelled to the enormous fum of 90,000l. In the moft expenfive year of the laft glorious war, under the councils and aufpices of the im-mortal Pitt, fecret fervice money never ex-ceeded 237,000l. from the prefent accounts they amounted to about 280,000l.

But the great difcovery to the Nation, of the fhameful neglect and fcandalous profufion of the prefent Government, and all the fecrets of contract jobbs, army ex-traordinaries, and contingencies, was made on the 15th of December, in the Houfe of Lords. By a deduction of facts and reafon-ing, that forced conviction on the minds of the moft venal and interefted, the Earl of Shelburne, on that day, enforced the bane-ful confequences that have flowed to this country from the boundlefs pecuniary in-fluence acquired by the crown ; the wanton diffipation of the public treafures in all the wicked modes of corruption ; the fhame-ful profufion in all the public offices ; the

enormous

enormous annual increafe of the army extraordinaries, voted as things of courfe,
without enquiry or account; the ingenuity
of the Minifter, in creating new employments for his inftruments at the public expence, and his barefaced devices for enrich-
ing his favourites with penfions drawn from
the induftry of an impoverifhed people.

On the comparative proportion between
the extraordinary military fervices of the
late war, with the prefent, he ftated the following alarming facts.

In the year 1757, the expences were but
800,000 l. thofe of 1777, including the
tranfport fervice, were 2,200,000 l.

In the year 1762, when our arms were
borne triumphant to every quarter of the
globe, when we had a force of eighty thoufand men in Germany, befides victorious
armies in North America, in the Britifh
and French Weft-Indies, in Eaft-India, in
Portugal, on the Coaft of France, at the
Havannah, the extraordinaries did not a-
mount to more than two millions. In the
difgraceful campaigns of 1778 and 1779,
they amounted to upwards of three millions each year: yet it was well known,
that œconomy was not the diftinguifhing
virtue of the Earl of Chatham.

From thefe facts he made it appear, that
in the four laft years of difgrace and defeat,
the very extra military expences would form
no lefs a fum than eight millions and a
half: a fum very nearly equal to the whole
expenditure of the four firft years of King

William.

William, and fully equal to the two firſt years of the great Marlborough's immortal campaigns.

In dragging to view the ſhameful arcanas of jobbs and contracts, he pointed out the difference between the conduct of former Miniſters and the preſent. During the laſt war, it was thought ſufficient to employ one contractor; the preſent Firſt Lord of the Treaſury multiplies the number to twelve. So many different friends are obliged by this expedient; ſo many aſſured votes are added to his influence.

During the laſt war, the Contractor was obliged to furniſh proviſion on the ſpot, in America, at ſixpence a ration, including all expences. What was the bargain with the preſent Contractors? To deliver rations at the ſame price in *Cork*. Freight, inſurance, riſque, all was taken from the pockets of the public, and beſtowed upon the friends of the Miniſter. Forty thouſand pounds were paid to one man, a Mr. Gordon, for ſuperintending the loading of the proviſions on board the victualling ſhips *.

From among the Favourites on whom the Miniſter laviſhed the plunder of the Public, Mr. Atkinſon was particularly brought forward. In the laſt four years, that gentleman's contract amounted to one million ſeven hun-

* This man charged no leſs a ſum than 5000l. for carting, though the merchants in Cork loaded the lighters at their warehouſe doors; nor was a ſingle car or cart ever uſed for the purpoſe. This fact muſt not have been known to his Lordſhip, as he made no mention of it.

dred

dred thoufand pounds. One of thefe was made for five thoufand hogfheads of rum, at a price actually double to what it could be purchafed for on the quays of London. A committee of merchants, trading to the Weft Indies, had examined this Contract, difapproved it, and reported accordingly to the Commons; yet not a fingle ftep had ever been taken to make the fraudulent Contractor refund. On the contrary, he was again trufted by the Minifter, and continues to receive greater favours than any other of the tribe.

Mr. Alderman Harley, was next diftinguifhed. This gentleman had tranfmitted to America, no lefs a fum than three millions feven hundred thoufand pounds, for the ufe of the troops; yet, in pretending to account for it to the Commons, he had not produced a fingle voucher. The paper he prefented, confifted of ftatements of fuch capital fums as forty and thirty thoufand pounds in a lump, without any fpecification whatever, how or in what manner, or to what ufe they were applied.

When it appeared that millions were thus iffued from the Treafury, without any reftraint or controul, and that the Reprefentatives of the People neglected to require the leaft account of them, was it to be wondered at, if the army extraordinaries fhould have become, what the noble Earl called them, the Civil Lift of the Minifter, and filled up the bottomlefs gulph of fecret fervice-money? Could it be any longer a fecret

cret from what fource the venality of Parliament drew the purchafe of its pliability, and fubferviency to the Minifter of Finance? Could there be a doubt to what caufe we fhould attribute the calamities, which a profligate Adminiftration had been enabled to entail upon this country?

The prodigality of the Commons in their blind and unconditional grants to the endlefs claims of the Civil-lift, to fallacious eftimates, arbitrary extraordinaries and contingencies, fupplied matter for the prodigality of the Minifter. They granted in order to be paid. Their boundlefs profufion was at once the caufe and effect of that enormous influence of the Crown, to which all our grievances are to be attributed. It was a fund of corruption, that multiplied as faft as the exigencies, real or pretended, of the ftate required, an addition of taxes and impofitions. Under its encouragement, the very errors of Adminiftration, and the ruinous confequences of the meafures purfued by an iniquitous Minifter, widened the circle of his influence. The enemies he armed againft his country, the poffeffions of which he ftripped her, the refources he cut off, and alienated from her for ever, furnifhed him with new claims to opprefs, to impoverifh, to exhauft her. He laid his rapacious hands on her with impunity, becaufe the fund to which he owed his fafety was increafed by his rapacioufnefs, and his crimes, while they accumulated, became his fecurity.

After having conveyed fuch fullnefs of
infor-

information to the Houfe, Lord Shelburne was well warranted to call on all the friends of the Conftitution to join with him in checking an evil, which, in the prefent dangerous pofture of affairs, threatened the State with immediate diffolution. Well might he conjure them to join the men, with whom he was connected, in adopting a fyftem of rigid œconomy fuited to our impoverifhed condition. But, alas! how could he hope for fuccefs in the refult of fuch a motion within thofe polluted walls? How could thofe, who toiled for the fame purpofe among the Commons, hope for it? Fenced in with the very places, penfions, contracts and emoluments, which their fyftem undertook to fave to the Public, the Minifters *voted* their accufations to be groundlefs, without attempting to refute them, and *proved* their own innocence, by fetting their face againft every propofal for an enquiry.

While this important queftion was debating among the Lords, Mr. Burke was zealoufly engaged in pleading the caufe of the People before their Reprefentatives. He lamented that the defire of fome œconomical reformation in the public expenditure operated every where but where it ought to operate moft powerfully. Thofe to whom the Conftitution had entrufted the exclufive management of the public purfe, were the only perfons who did not feem to have turned their thoughts that way. The cry for œconomy refounded in the ftreets and high ways. Thefe complaints of the People were

an

an accusation against their Representatives.
The Lords had taken the lead, and the pro-
sitions lately made by the Duke of Richmond, and those which were that very day
making by Lord Shelburne, were a reproach
to them.

From Administration, not a single ex-
pression had dropped on this subject of
œconomy; they had not even thrown an
oblique hint which glanced that way. In-
dustry and ingenuity were put to the stretch
to find taxes to support the war. The Minister suggested, planned, adopted, yet, in
all his begettings and adoptings, in all his
schemes practicable and impracticable, he
never once thought of Oeconomy.

Our enemies might have instructed him
better. The war, on the side of France,
was a war of œconomy, the most dreadful
of all wars. Monsieur Neckar, the French
Minister of finance, could boast that he had
brought his fixed and certain expences to
an equilibrium with his receipts. In those
fixed expences, he reckoned an annual sink-
ing of debt. For the additional services of
the war, he borrowed only two millions. He
borrowed not for perpetuity, but for lives;
and not a single tax was levied on the subject
to fund that loan. The great fund, from
which he meant to draw the interest, was
œconomy, improvement of the public revenue, and the abolition of unnecessary places.

The propositions towards our enemy in
the other House had been rejected by Ministers. There was every reason to fear
they

they would equally combat every propofition of the fame tendency from the Commons. But though they oppofed, what it
was their duty to promote, and what their
place gave them the power of effecting, yet
the important bufinefs would not be left
unattempted. It fhould be brought into
the Houfe. He fhould himfelf fubmit a
plan to the confideration of Parliament after the recefs, that would partly tend to
fatisfy the wifhes and defires of the People.
He fhould be fupported by a fet of men in
both Houfes, to whofe union this fyftem
formed an indiffoluble cement, and who
would ftrenuoufly and unanimoufly direct
all their labours to the fame defirable end.
The defect of power fhould be made up by
fidelity and diligence. They relied on the
affiftance of the People; if they were not
true to themfelves, it was not in the power
of any fet of men, however zealous and
well inclined to fave them.

The accumulating fufferings of the People, and the loudnefs of their clamours, extorted from them by the oppreffive grievances
under which they laboured, gave undoubted affurances of this fupport. The Genius
of England began to ftir itfelf in the North.
The attention of the whole kingdom was
directed towards its motions. It dictated
the refolutions of the affembly of the Freeholders at York, and its animating fpirit
foon diffufed itfelf through moft of the
counties of England. A deep and univerfal alarm feized Minifters and their adhe-

H   rents

rents. They were attacked in their ſtrong
hold. The conteſt was not only for their
ſafety, but for their lives. All the forces of
government were called out. Their emiſſa-
ries were diſperſed through every part of the
country. Power and falſhood, intereſt and
miſrepreſentation, threats and promiſes,
went hand in hand, through the kingdom,
to corrupt, to divide, to miſlead, to weaken,
by any and every means, to defeat a combination, that threatened to reſcue the nation from their hands. In ſome counties, they acted by their agents ; in others,
they toiled in perſon. Rewards were held
out to the zealous, threats to the luke-
warm, and puniſhments to the * refractory.
But the ſucceſs fell far ſhort of their ſtrain-
ings and ſtretchings, in this favourite cauſe

* The Lords, Pembroke and Carmarthen, were removed from their places for their conduct on this occaſion. A Nobleman of a different character, who exerted all his powers to defeat the Petitions, has been
ſince rewarded with one of thoſe places, the abolition of
which he oppoſed with ſuch *prudent* zeal, he is now
Treaſurer of his Majeſty's Houſhold.. After this, let the
tools of the Miniſter preſume to impoſe on the Public by
invidiouſly attributing the zeal of Oppoſition to their
envy of the places enjoyed by the friends of Adminiſtration. The one labour night and day, they exert all their
intereſt to aboliſh thoſe places ; the others unite all their
perſonal powers, all their influence to preſerve them,
and in reward, enjoy them at the expence of an impoveriſhed People. The abolition of thoſe places is an
indiſpenſible condition, without which the leaders of
Oppoſition *have refuſed* to undertake the government
(for the offer has been made 'to them) ; the preſervation of
thoſe places is a neceſſary requiſite to the continuance of
the preſent Miniſtry.

of corruption. The sense of the public misery, and the feelings of the People,, bore down even their almighty influence. By the meeting of Parliament more than one hundred thousand Freeholders had petitioned for an immediate reformation in the public expenditure. The Table of the House of Commons presented a spectacle that could not fail of being highly grateful to every Englishman. It was restored at length to the pious uses for which it was raised by our ancestors. It was become once more the Altar of the People. Piled with their sacred instructions, the nation looked up to it, as to the shrine, from which alone they expected their salvation.

The first of the Petitions that made its way into the House, was the Petition of the Freeholders of the county of York. It was presented by the most incorruptible hands that ever conveyed the grave and solemn sentiments of an assembled People to their Representatives. The importance of the subject, and the anxious expectation of an oppressed Public, had drawn together the fullest attendance of Members and strangers that had ever been known. We were struck with a new (and for many years) an unhoped-for scene. It made its impression even on the Treasury-bench. We lost sight of that haughty, confident air, with which they had so long been accustomed to survey their Band of Mercenaries.

A deep silence, and a fixed attention prevailed on both sides of the House, and inspired

the

the moſt trifling minds with awe and reſpect, when Sir George Savile roſe, and laying
his hand on the Petition, expreſſed the ſenti-
ments of 8000 of his Conſtituents.

The object of their prayer was an enquiry into the public expenditure. The di-
miniſhed reſources and growing burdens of
the country, had convinced them that the
ſtricteſt frugality was indiſpenſably necef-
ſary in every department of the State. They
long had obſerved with grief, that notwith-
ſtanding the calamitous and impoveriſhed
condition of the Nation, much public money had been improvidently ſquandered;
that many individuals enjoyed ſinecure
places, efficient places with exorbitant emoluments, and penſions unmerited by public ſervices, to a large and ſtill increaſing
amount. The danger reſulting from this
evil to the Nation was not confined to the
mere bad conſequences which muſt necef-
ſarily flow from unbounded profuſion; it
was the ſource of that unconſtitutional influence of the Crown, which, if not check-
ed, might ſoon prove fatal to the Liberties
of this country. They appealed to the
juſtice of their Repreſentatives, to whoſe
cuſtody the national purſe was in a peculiar
manner entruſted, and they intreated them,
that before any new burdens were laid upon
the country, effectual meaſures might be taken
by the Houſe, to enquire into and correct the
groſs abuſe in the expenditure of the public
money; to reduce all exorbitant emoluments,
to reſcind and aboliſh all ſinecure places and
unmerited

unmerited penfions ; and to appropriate the produce to the neceffities of the State in fuch manner as to the wifdom of Parliament fhould feem meet.

" Thefe (faid Sir George) are the great
" objects to which 8000 of my Conftituents
" exprefsly inftruct this Houfe to direct
" their immediate attention. They are re-
" prefented calmly and with moderation.
" Nothing is faid of the conduct of Minif-
" ters ; no ftrictures are made on their paft
" meafures ; the moft pointed care has been
" taken to fhun all appearance of party.
" They ground their application on the too
" manifeft and acknowledged calamities
" with which the Nation is furrounded.
" They do not take upon themfelves to dictate
" any particular mode of enquiry or redrefs
" of the grievances of which they complain.
" They do not inftruct Parliament where
" they are to go, or what particular fteps
" they are to take. They only expect, from
" the wifdom and integrity of the Repre-
" fentatives of the People, that they fhall
" not be put off with palliatives, excufes,
" fhuffling artifices, partial expedients. ---
" Mock enquiries will not anfwer their ex-
" pectations.

" Miniftry I know, continued he, will
" not dare to refufe to give the petition a
" hearing. But it may be an eafy matter,
" with fuch Minifters, to hear a Petition,
" while they fecretly refolve not to comply
" with the prayer of it."

Before

Before I proceed to give an account of the subsequent proceedings of Parliament, and of the shameful and flagitious expedients, the palliatives, the excuses, the shuffling artifices, the partial expedients, by which the Minister verified the hints thrown out by Sir George Savile on the success of this and the other petitions, I shall briefly state some concomitant circumstances that are essential to the proper information of the Public.

The Petitions intreated, that before any additional taxes should be levied on the country, an enquiry should be instituted into the expenditure of the produce of those already laid. The Minister began his inimical opposition, by declaring his intentions of postponing every consideration of the Petitions to that of ways and means for raising the supplies. When Ireland had applied for a redress of her grievances, she began by voting a short money bill. Till her prayer should be heard, and her petition for a free trade granted, she refused to raise any further supplies. This conduct was admired, applauded by the Minister, and he granted her demands in reward of her public virtue. But the People of England had, it seems, no claim to such indulgence. There was one law for the Associations of Ireland, and another for the Assemblies of the Freeholders of England. But the difference was obvious—The *Parliament* of Ireland adopted the language of its Constituents;—the Parliament of England,

land, it was well known to the Minifter, would facrifice their Conftituents to his continuance in office.

I have already hinted at the alarm into which the firft report of the Petitions threw the Miniftry and their adherents, and the various arts and unconftitutional attempts they made ufe of to defeat their defigns. Among thefe, the moft daring was the removal of the Earl of Pembroke and Lord Carmarthen from the employments they held under the Crown. This event took place fome time after the prefent period; but I fhall take notice of it here, that it may not interrupt the narrative of the bufinefs of the Petitions.

The Marquis of Carmarthen, a young nobleman of the greateft hopes, was Lord-lieutenant of the Eaft Riding of York, and Chamberlain to her Majefty. But he poffef-fed thofe places with that fpirit of Independence, with which nice principles of honour, and an attachment to the Conftitution may naturally be fuppofed to infpire a young man, the dignity of whofe fentiments was equal to the high rank he was born to fill in the State. He would have thought him-felf difgraced by any mark of the royal favour, that would require the facrifice of the duty he owed his country. When, therefore, he began to weigh with himfelf the miferies that hung over thefe Kingdoms, fhould the meafures purfued by the prefent Servants of the Crown continue to be fup-ported, he refolved to withdraw from them, and

and to unite with the men, to whom he en-
vied the boaſt of having uniformly oppoſed
a ſyſtem of which he had not, till then, per-
ceived all the ruinous effects. To the diſ-
guſt, occaſioned at Court by the avowal of
theſe intentions, was added a public letter,
written to the Chairman of the Yorkſhire
Petitions, wherein he expreſſed his approbation of the principles of the County Petitions, and the conviction he felt of the neceſſity of the reformation they were deſign-
ed to effect. The conſequence was the re-
ſignation of his Chamberlain's Staff, and
his immediate diſmiſſion from the Lieute-
nancy of the Eaſt Riding.

The anceſtors of the Earl of Pembroke
had been Lords Lieutenant of Wiltſhire
ever ſince that office was known in England.
His Lordſhip was remarkably popular in
the County, and his conduct, upon all oc-
caſions, had been ſuch as to merit that popularity. But he voted, on the 8th of February, for Lord Shelburne's motion, for a
commiſſion of public accounts, and in a
few days after he was removed from his employment of Lord Lieutenant, without re-
ceiving any reaſon whatever for ſuch a mark
of his Sovereign's diſpleaſure.

The ſevereſt marks of diſapprobation, under the influence of the preſent Councils, could
be no diſgrace to men of their high ſpirits and
elevated ſtations. But they deeply reſented
the blow that was ſtruck through them at
the dignity of Peerage, the freedom of debate, and the independency of Parliament.

But the mifchievous councils of the minifter looked much further than even this
daring attempt on the independency of parliament. The militia was originally infti-
tuted as a conftitutional force, and pointed
to two objects; to be a defence to the Kingdom againft our foreign enemies, and that
this defence might be compofed of men not
immediately dependent on the crown and
its minifters. But the conftitution of it had
of late years undergone a total change. Unqualified perfons had been permitted to ferve,
merely as mercenaries, in confideration of
pay and rank. Inftead of the men drafted
from the different parifhes, fubftitutes had
been received, and continued to ferve beyond
the three years for which they had engaged.
Additional companies had been raifed in moft
counties, exactly in the fame mode, and on
the fame terms that regulars beat up for re-
cruits. The militia by thefe means differed
very little from the ftanding army; one only
fecurity was left to the kingdom; the controul
of the lieutenants of the feveral counties. In
difmiffing thefe two noblemen from that office,
the minifter had taken the firft ftep to withdraw that fecurity alfo. If lieutenants were
fuffered to be difmiffed, merely for their political principles, and for exerting that inherent right of the conftitution, of fpeaking
with freedom, and voting according to their
confcience, pretences would never be wanting, as they could be continually created, for
difplacing poffeffors of that great truft of one

I   defcrip-

defcription, and replacing them by others of more pliant principles. By thefe means it would be a much lefs difficult tafk to manage the militia than the army; and the minifter would find the provincial force much more fubfervient to his wifhes than the eftablifhed.

One would have imagined that an attack on the very vitals of the conftitution, of fuch complicated guilt, and extenfive dangerous tendency, would have united the whole body of the reprefentatives in imprecating cenfure on the advifers of it; but the Commons did not make a fingle effort to interpofe the authority of the people. The independent Lords, indeed, inveighed in the Upper Houfe againft fo direct and formal a violation of their privileges, with the indignation it deferved. They moved a vote of cenfure againft the advifers of fo dangerous a ftretch of his majefty's prerogative; but as ufual, they found corruption and influence too powerful a match for the pride of birth, dignity, and confequence. They were outnumbered, and the minifter was protected, even in fo glaring an inftance of arbitrary and unconftitutional proceedings, by ninety-two peers againft thirty-nine.

The laft meafure of the minifter which I fhall confider under this head, is the *the protefts* which he laboured to procure againft the petitioners. The methods he employed to induce the deluded people to fign thefe inftruments of their own flavery, would form

as

as black a page as any in the records of his infamous adminiſtration.

The very principles of the proteſts was a renunciation of the firſt privilege of an Engliſhman,—the right of petitioning parliament. They declared the exerciſe of that right to be unconſtitutional. They branded the meetings held for the purpoſe of exerciſing it, with the imputation of ſedition and rebellion. Every mean, invidious, oppreſſive expedient of force and artifice, threats and allurements, were put in practice to procure numbers to ſign them. Letters were ſent round to every man connected with adminiſtration, deſiring him to ſtay away from the county meetings, and to exert all his influence in preventing the attendance of others: a conduct the moſt daſtardly that ever men, in the hour of their timidity could ſtoop to; —that betrayed a baſe fear, a conſcious dread of enquiry; the influence of which could ariſe only in meanneſs of heart.

On ſome the proteſts were paſſed for the petitions. By this ſhameful impoſition, many were beguiled to ſet their names to them, who afterwards declared that they would have loſt their right hand, rather than have ſigned a proteſt againſt a petition praying for œconomy.

How different were theſe proteſts from the petitions? the petitioners, with all decency and reſpect, carried their complaints before their repreſentatives. From them alone they ſupplicated redreſs; from their legal inter-

ference

ference alone they hoped for relief. They made thier grievances known in the face of the legiflature, according to the eftablifhed modes of the conftitution, in a form that would neceffarily procure them a *public* hearing. But what was the conduct of the proteftors? How did minifters direct them to proceed? (for the meafure originated from the cabinet.) Did they apply to parliament? Did they offer any counter petitions? Did they fpecify any reafons why they thought the prayer of the petitions fhould not be granted? The very atrempt to offer their protefts to parliament, was fcouted by every fide of the houfe, as an object of the moft palpable fcorn and contempt*. Mr. Smith however, *reluctantly, yet* in obedience even to fo fmall a part of his electors, propofed to read this proteft to the houfe. The minifter himfelf was the moft hearty in joining in the laugh, that the very attempt inftantly fpread from the fpeaker's chair to the Treafury-Bench, from the Treafury-Bench to the Gallery.

By this it too plainly appeared, that thofe infiduous inftruments, hatched in darknefs and privacy, produced in corners and byeways, fed by cunning and menace, were meant to have effect, not within doors, but without. It was but too obvious that they were meant not to convey to parliament the

fenfe

* It was in the cafe of the Nottingham petitition, figned by fix of the burgeffes.

fenfe of their conftituents, not to quiet the
minds of the moderate and peaceably inclined,
as was pretended, not to carry proper information to the throne, but to raife the flames
of fedition, which miniftry affected to dread ;
to fpread abroad that feditious fpirit which*
minifters had the audacity to impute to the
favourers of the Affociations; to divide the
people into parties and factions, and to arm
them againft each other; to deceive parliament, to impofe on the fovereign, and to
keep the genuine cries of his oppreffed fubjects from reaching his ears.

Mr. *Burke's Bill for regulating the Civil Lift.*

The firft attempt that was made in the
Houfe of Commons, to obtain the object of the county petitions, was, on the
eleventh of February. On that memorable
day,

* Lord Hillfborough, in a tranfport of that furious zeal
that firft denounced the vengeance of adminiftration againft
the devoted colonies, and tore afunder the ties between the
two countries, branded thefe humble and dutiful petitions
of the people, to be relieved from the heavy burthens under which they laboured, *as factious, and founded merely in
a fpirit of violence and party.* The conftitutional meetings
for conveying the fentiments of the conftituents to their
reprefentatives, he maintained to be *dangerous, difloyal, feditious combinations, evidently tending to rebellion.* Lord
Mulgrave ufed nearly the fame language, but added,
that the *promoters of them fhould be punifhed with juftice, but
without pity.*

day, memorable as long as integrity ſhall
challenge veneration, or talents command ap-
plauſe, Mr. Burke introduced his plan for
the better ſecurity of the independance of
Parliament, and the œconomical reformation
of the civil and other eſtabliſhments.

This was not a dream of ſpeculation, a
phantom blown up to dazzle and deceive.
It was calculated " to include in its execu-
" tion a conſiderable reduction of improper
" expence;, to effect a converſion of unpro-
" fitable titles into a productive eſtate; to
" lead to, and indeed almoſt compel a pro-
" vident adminiſtration of ſuch ſums of
" public money as muſt remain under diſ-
" cretionary truſts; to render the incurring
" debts on the civil eſtabliſhment, which
" muſt ultimately affect national ſtrength
" and national credit, ſo very difficult as to
" become next to impracticable*."

But

---

* The Earl of Shelburne had, on the 8th of February,
introduced his motion for a committee of accounts.
But miniſtry threw it out by a majority of 101 to 55.
The minority lords entered, on this occaſion, the ſtrongeſt
proteſt that ever appeared on the books of the Houſe. It
is ſigned by thirty-five of the wealthieſt, and moſt diſtinguiſhed peers of the realm. It contains a ſtatement
of the melancholy grounds on which the motion was
framed, and the reaſons for preſſing it upon the houſe.
It records the moſt palpable inſtances of the profligacy
and profuſion with which the public treaſures have been
laviſhed, without examination or accounts. It anſwers
all the objections that were urged againſt the motion,
in the courſe of the debate, and will remain for ever an
authentic

But what this eloquent fpeaker, and incorruptible ftatefman " bent the whole force
" of his mind to, was the reduction of that
" corrupt influence, which is itfelf the pe-
" renial fpring of all prodigality, and of
" all diforder; which loads us more than
" millions of debts which takes away vigour
" from our arms, wifdom from our coun-
" cils, and every fhadow of authority and
" credit from the moft venerable parts of
" our conftitution."

The moderation and candour, the extent
and variety of information, the depth of
judgement, the perfpecuity of reafoning, and
the elegance of manner with which this
plan was introduced, extorted the warmeft
and moft unreferved applaufe, even from his
enemies. I mean, from the enemies of his
country; for they alone can be enemies to
this truly great and amiable man. The
minifter was himfelf the firft to extol it
above all the poffible productions of the moft
brilliant characters within the circle of his
knowledge. But under the infidious veil of
this unbounded approbation, he concealed
the defign he has fince unhappily executed,
of defeating all the falutary purpofes of the
plan.

authentic monument of the degeneracy of the prefent
Houfe of Lords, who could deny their bleeding country
the relief this motion held out to it; and who could facrifice their duty to the defence of a fet of men, againft
whom fuch crimes and mifdemeanors were thus authenticated?

plan. He honoured the whole of the propofitions it contained, with an effufion of compliments; but when each diftinct part came under confideration, he oppofed, he he condemned, he rejected it; and though in the progrefs of the bill he fuffered a few of the claufes to pafs at different ftages, he afterwards took care, when he had compleatly triumphed over the decency and honour of the houfe, to have them thrown out.

Sir George Savile's Motion for the Penfion Lift.

This plan of Mr. Burke's was followed on the 21ft of the fame month by a motion of Sir George Saville's to addrefs his Majefty, that he would be gracioufly pleafed to give directions, that there be laid before the houfe an account of all fubfifting penfions granted by the crown during pleafure, or otherwife; fpecifying the amount of fuch penfions refpectively, and the times when, and the perfons to whom fuch penfions were granted.

This motion went directly to the great object of the petitions of the people. They had prayed that penfions, unmerited by public fervices, all finecure places, or efficient places with exhorbitant fallaries fhould be retrenched, and the favings appropriated to the public fervice. But without an authentic

lift

lift of the perfons enjoying fuch penfions, it would be impoffible to appreciate their refpective merits, or obtain the information neceffary to comply with the requifitions of the people, in the full and manifeft fenfe of their application. There could be no other means of gaining a certain knowledge of the fums fquandered away in that fcandalous traffic.

This motion gave rife to one of the moft extraordinary debates that ever was heard in a legiflative affembly. As it will afford one of the ftrongeft criterions by which the people can judge of the conduct of their reprefentatives, it will be neceffary to be more particular and circumftantial in my account of it.

The Minifter had neither the virtue to acknowledge the juftice of the motion, nor the courage to reject it. It went fo clearly and decifively to the prayer of the petitions, that he did not dare to get rid of it by an abfolute and unqualified negative. He was at the fame time defirous of giving his creatures fome colour able excufe, for fupporting him in fo pofitive an oppofition to the demands of their conftituents. He therefore moved an amendment, which feemed to pay fome attention to the requefts of the people, but which in fact, defeated all the falutary effects that could be expected from the motion, as it came pure from the mouth of the virtuous mover, and unadulterated by this ftate-craft.

K   He

He was called upon to submit to the consideration of Parliament, a list of *all* pensions,
and he proposes, by his amendment, to produce two, which he says, must content the
people.

What were those lists? the one was the
the list of pensions payable at the Exchequer.
The other is the private pensions, or what
he called, Lord Gage's List.

The amount of these, he said, had been
already presented to the House, on an application to Parliament for an encrease of the
civil establishment.

In the list of private pensions, he refused
to specify names; they lay at the public
office, they might be seen by any one who
chose to apply for them.

He refused to specify the seperate sums,
as paid to individuals; the total amount must
satisfy the Parliament and the people. If
there were any abuses, any improper persons,
or any sums undefervedly granted, to be
found on either of the lists, the gentlemen
of the opposition should point them out, and
not *suspect* where they could not *arraign.*

These were what the minister was pleased
to call his unanswerable arguments against
the motion; let us see on what grounds they
stood.

The virtuous and independent among the
representative body, agreeable to the instructions of their constituents, call for information.
The minister, with all the appearance of can-

dour

dour and condefcenfion, tells them they fhall have it; but how will he acquit himfelf of this promife? he will give them fuch information as they have already had, and which they confequently do not want. For this information had been already given, and the two lifts he propofed to produce at the requeft of the people of England, had been laid before Parliament on an application of his own, for an encreafe of the civil lift.

But the information which could alone fatisfy the doubts, and meet the expectations of the people — the information that could alone bring properly to light what, or if any individuals enjoyed finecure places, efficient places with exorbitant emoluments, and penfions unmerited by public fervices, that they fhould not have. Nay, one of his oratorical fupporters, the Lord Advocate of Scotland, had the audacity to declare, in the full hearing of the houfe, members and ftrangers, that the petitioners did not want that information. Words could not be more precife or explicit, than thofe which the petitioners had ufed to recommend fuch an enquiry; yet this gentleman, with all the fire of his zeal, did not hefitate to affirm, that if they were called to the bar, they would, one and all declare, that the penfion-lift was not one of the objects of their complaints. How low, abject and fervile muft the reprefentatives of the people have been in the eyes of that man, to encourage him to offer fuch arguments to them by way of influencing their votes!

But

' But why not produce the names of the
' private lift ? faid the friends of the people.'—
It would not be right. It would not be
delicate.—It would be fubjecting the penfioners to the flanderous comments of news-paper
writers, and the dealers in fcandal. Their
honor and their peace of mind might be de-
ftroyed, by fo unfeeling a difcovery. So ten-
derly did his Majefty's confidential fervant
feel for the *honor* of his penfioners ; but for
the people of England he had no feelings.
The miferies of the public could not be redreffed, they fhould be eternal, if they could
only be removed at the expence of the peace
of mind of *his* friends.

" But there was no neceffity to produce
" them ; if the people wanted to be fatisfied,
" they might apply to Lord Gage's office,
" and there they fhould find them."

So contemptible were the unanimous petitions of the people of England, in the eftimation of this infolent minifter ! to gratify
their wifhes, he would not even condefcend,
officially to fubmit to their reprefentatives, a lift
which he infinuated, might be procured by any
unauthorized perfon who would take the trou-
ble to call for it. The wifhes of the kingdom
at large, might be gratified by fo trifling a
mark of his attention ; yet he exerted all his
powers, he called together his moft trufty adherents, and fought at their head, as for his
very exiftence, to prevent being compelled to
grant this indulgence.

If

If the names on that lift were fuch as fhould
command the approbation of the public; if
they were fuch as had indifputable claims on
the gratitude and liberality of a generous nation, for fervices performed; if there were no
fears that any fhould be found among them,
who blufhed not to add to their princely for-
tunes fome miferable ftipend, fqueezed from
the toils and fweat of the people; if there
were none who received the infamous wages
of a filent vote, without the fhadow of a merit,
or even a pretence of public fervice; if there
were none who could be fufpected to have
been hired* to libel every friend of the people,
to turn every thing that fhould be held facred
and venerable by Englifhmen into ridicule,
to brand all pretentions to patriotifm, or the
love of ones country with mockery and fcorn,
openly to attack the moft invaluable liberties
of the fubject, and to revive, under the reign
of a Brunfwick, the arbitrary doctrines and
high prerogative principles of a Stewart—If
the minifter had no fears of this nature, why
not produce the lift?— The people would
be undeceived—The odium that was meant
to be brought upon his *immaculate* adminiftration, would recoil upon thofe who de-
vifed it.

He

* No lefs a fum than one thoufand pounds a year, are
paid *in penfions* to the editor and eftablifhed writers of
the Morning Poft.

He proceeded—" The fums are trifling.
" They are no object—They fhould be lefs
" than nothing in the eftimation of a great
" and wealthy people."——

But to what did thefe arguments tend?
To the giving a negative to every feperate ar-
ticle as it occurred in the detail of this important bufinefs, and fo effectually defeating
the general reform. But how did he prove
that the fums were trifling? Did he dare to
aver that thefe were the only lifts which in-
gulphed the treafures of the public? Where
was the lift drawn up in darknefs, and under
all the terrors of fhame and guilt, which was
no fooner prefented, approved and difcharged,
than it was committed to the flames, and the
very afhes of it fcattered abroad to the winds——
The lift of thofe members of parliament, who,
at the end of every feffion received the wages
of their fervile acquiefcence to minifters,
and their treachery to their conftituents?
How many were there at that inftant in the
houfe, whofe criminating eyes would meet
the minifter's if he attempted to deny the exiftence of fuch a lift?—Where was the lift of
fecret fervice money? Where was the lift paid
from the privy purfe? Were the fums to
which all thefe amount, *trifling*, and below
the attention of a great and wealthy people?

Or was the amount of thefe fums the only
confideration that induced the freeholders to
demand a general reformation. Were there
no

no conſtitutional conſiderations blended with their requiſitions for œconomy ? Did the abolition of the dangerous and deſtructive influence which the miniſter purchaſed by thoſe penſions, trifling as they were, form no part in the object of the county petitions ? Was the ſum to which Mr. Hampden was taxed for his portion of ſhip-money, the only motive that induced him to reſiſt that unconſtitutional impoſition ?

Such was the main purport of the arguments on both ſides, when a majority of the houſe ſupported the amendment of the miniſter, and enabled him to refuſe to gratify the wiſhes of the people, or to grant them even a hope of redreſs. The worthy member from whom the motion originated, diſclaimed it with its amendment. It could not convey to his conſtituents the information, he thought it his duty to procure them. It could furniſh no grounds for obtaining for them that relief which was his object in making the motion.

The Miniſter's Commiſſion of Accounts Bill.

This motion of Sir George Saville being thus diſpoſed of, a bill was introduced, in conſequence of the petitions, on a ſide of the houſe, from whence nothing could be expected, but that ſcene of deceit, fallacy, and colluſion, to which the only meaſure that has been granted even in pretence to the prayers of the

people

people gave rife. Col. Barré had given notice to the houfe, that on a certain day, he intended to bring in leave for a bill to appoint a commiffion for an inveftigation into the expenditure of the public accounts. He meant it, he faid, as an effential part of that reform, which was the object of the county petitions, and he was in hopes it would tend to the fame falutary purpofes which his friend, Mr. Burke, propofed to the public by the plan he had exhibited.

He entreated the concurrence of the minifter, he fhewed him his plan.—It had his approbation—He promifed it all the fupport of his authority, and the affiftance of office*.

Yet to the utter aftonifhment of the houfe, in a manner unprecedented in the annals of parliament, by a device which would have difgraced any man who pretends to the character of a gentleman, the minifter came

down

Col. Barré, in the courfe of his fpeech, on the 21ft of March, gave a moft ftriking account to the houfe of the trick and impofition, with which this bufinefs was managed. " I called upon gentlemen faid he, in the ref-
" pective offices at the Exchequer, and preffed expidition
" in making out the accounts called for. I called at the au-
" ditor's ; they directed me to *the* chamberlain, the cham-
" berlain to the pells, the pells to the teller's, and fo on
" *ad infinitum*. When I endeavoured to make myfelf
" underftood, they refpectively ftared, and feemed fur-
" prifed, and alternately fhifted me off from one to the
" other, till I was inclined to believe that the requeft I had
" made of the noble lord, was only agreed to in order to
" render me ridiculous to the clerks in office."

down on the fecond of March, and propofed a commiffion of accounts, framed by himfelf for the purpofe of this enquiry.

Several circumftances had concurred to compel him to adopt this infulting meafure. The loud voice of the people had begun to make an evident impreffion within doors as it had done without. A formal and declared oppofition to their requefts might fhake even a power more firm and eftablifhed than that which the obfequious complaifance of parliament had enabled him to acquire. He had juft difcovered a defection in a quarter from which he had long derived an authorative fupport. The fhamelefs inconfiftency and unblufhing duplicity of his conduct, joined to a confideration of the fatal confequences of his meafures, had given difguft to the fpeaker, and that able and experienced fenator had thrown all the weight of his abilities and knowledge into the fcale of the people.

In thefe circumftances, a commiffion of accounts with retrofpective powers to enquire into paft abufes, and confifting of great and independent characters, without the magic circle of his influence, boded the moft fearful confequences. If he fuffered the gentlemen who favoured the wifhes of the people to introduce a bill for that purpofe, they would have the power of prefcribing the objects of the enquiry, and propofing the members who fhould compofe the com-

L   mittee.

mittee. Nothing, therefore, was left for him but to take the meafure into his own hands, to introduce a bill bearing a fpecious title, and feemingly in compliance with the prayer of the petitions. Thus at once to fteal fome little popularity, and guard againft the apprehenfions he had fo juftly conceived on the firft propofal of the meafure.

Thus what he was fearful of attempting by force, he effected by ftratagem. But what could the Sicilians hope, when the redrefs of their grievances was configned to Verres? What profpect of relief was left to the petitioners when their caufe was thus fnatched from the hands of the honeft members who had introduced their petitions, cherifhed and fupported them, to be infolently taken up by a fet of men who had repeatedly fpurned and contemned them as factious and the bafe fpawn of fedition? How could they hope to have their grievances examined into, and redreffed by the very men who contended that they only exifted in the diftempered vifions and frantic ravings of popular madnefs?

This folemn mockery of the public was received by the majority of the reprefentatives, as all other mandates of the minifter have been received. We have feen it carried into execution; we have heard it claimed as a merit by the minifter; it has been urged as an inconteftable proof of his willingnefs to hear the people. But how does the matter
really

really ftand? Parliament has confented to delegate the moft facred truft they had received from the people, into the hands of the creatures of the minifter. They have fubmitted to the moft intollerable infult that was ever offered to the Commons of Great Britain. In the moft debafing manner to themfelves, and with the utmoft injuftice to their electors, they have fuffered their beft privilege to be annihilated.

The conftitution had vefted the infpection of the public accounts in the reprefentatives of the people exclufively. By this act of the minifter's, it is transferred to a fet of men, of whom the people have no knowledge, in whom they can have no truft, of whom they can have no bond of fecurity, no feal of certainty that they will faithfully and honeftly difcharge their duty. By thus betraying the confidence repofed in them by their conftituents, they have parted with half the power of the purfe, and the tranfition from this to the giving up the power of *voting* the public money, is not very difficult.

In the firft ftage of the bill, the minifter pledged himfelf, that the perfons he would nominate fhould have neither place, penfion, nor employment. Yet the very firft man whom he dared to offer to the houfe, was a creature of his own, poffeffing an employment under him. Not even the infolence with which the fervility of parliament had infpired him, could perfevere in this attempt.

L 2

But though he confented to withdraw the name of Mr. Bowlby *, yet the lift, which has been confirmed by the fanction of both houfes, prefents an authenticated violation of his faith, and an irrefragable teftimony of that corrupt influence, to which Parliament has fold the glory and intereft of their country.

In the fyftem lately adopted for the regulation of the army; men have been taken from the defk and placed at the head of regiments. In appointing the commiffioners, they have been taken from the head of regiments, and placed behind the defk. General Carleton, whofe great military talents might have been happily exerted in the fervice of his country, has been recalled from his command in Canada, with every aggravation of ill ufage and infult. But to make him amends, he is put at the head of a commiffion, that requires a turn of talents, and a line of practice to which, from his former habits he muft be an utter ftranger. Add to this, that he is himfelf very largely concerned in the accounts he is appointed to infpect.

Expedition in fettling thefe accounts, would be one great means of giving fatisfaction to the public, and this the minifter profeffed he had himfelf in view when he form-

ed

---

* Mr. Bowlby has, fince that time, been appointed commiffary general to the army. A good encouragement to the reft of the minifter's lift, who have been confirmed by Parliament! are not thefe things palpable?

ed the lift of the commiffioners. Yet he has entrufted it chiefly to Mafters in Chancery. If the method to which thefe gentlemen are accuftomed in making up their own accounts be adopted by the reft of the commiffioners, there may not be a fingle veftige of this conftitution left by the time it can be expected that they will complete their bufinefs.

Can fuch a commiffion be called not only a commencement of œconomy, but an ample and fatisfactory compliance with the petitions of the People? Can fuch a commiffion put an end to the abufes originating from the influence of the crown? Can it check the profufion of the public expenditure, and can it prevent the impofitions of contractors? In what does it end? In altering the conftitution, and robbing Parliament of its inherent rights. In encreafing the influnce of the Crown, by creating new dependants on the minifter. In enabling him to defraud the public with greater fecurity and eafe, by empowering him to appoint ftewards, dependant on himfelf, to cheque and controul his accounts. In creating a new board, and inftead of leffening, encreafing the expences of the ftate.

Contractor's Bill.

The corrupt influence which the Crown has acquired in Parliament, was one of the principle

principle fubjects of the complaints of the people. To reftrain it, was the only way left to fave the conftitution, and refcue the ftate from ruin, and no method that could tend to effect that falutary purpofe was left unattempted by the friends of the country. Among the moft obvioufly neceffary of thofe attempts, a bill was introduced into the Houfe of Commons early in the feffions, for excluding contractors from being members of that Houfe.

In the midft of a war in which nothing, among all its unhappy circumftances, was more remarkable than the prodigality with which it was carried on, it was evident that the corrupt fupply of military arrangements tended, in a very extenfive degree, to increafe the Court influence in Parliament. Oppref-fed with actual impofitions, and terrified with the certain profpect of encreafing heavier burdens, the people could not receive a more fatisfactory proof of the willingnefs of their reprefentatives to grant them effectual relief, than by enacting, that none fhould have a power of laying thofe burdens who fhould have fuch an intereft in encreafing them as the contractors had.

The abufe of fraudulent contracts was one of the great caufes of the public diftrefs. Nothing thererefore could be more unfit, than that thofe who were the principal fubjects of complaint fhould fit as comptrollers of their own conduct. On thefe ftrong grounds the bill was introduced

into

into the Lower Houfe. Here it met with no oppofition. But the public were early prepared for the fate it was to prove by a fpeech of one of the Secretaries of State, among the Lords in a debate on the bill when it was firft introduced into their Houfe. He told the Peers, that the time was come, when the hereditary legiflators of the realm fhould exercife the powers they were vefted with from the conftitution. A *phrenzy of virtue*, he faid, began to fhew itfelf in the Houfe of Commons. The people *had run mad*, and the infection was gaining upon their reprefentatives. It would therefore be the duty of the Lords to interfere in their controuling capacity, *to ftand in the gap*, as he expreffed himfelf, and to prevent the other branch of the Legiflature from adopting a reformation that was only grounded on the vifionary complaints of an over pampered people. We were little furprifed, therefore, that it fhould have been fuffered to pafs through the Commons, without oppofition. The odium of defeating this effential reform was evidently referved for the Lords. Accordingly, on the 14th of April, when it was read to them for the fecond time, they did not blufh to ftand between their oppreffed county, and this firft ftep that was taken towards fupporting the independency, integrity and virture of Parliament. The privilege vefted in them by the conftitution, they availed themfelves of in the moft unconftitutional manner; in a queftion that related

folely

folely to the interior regulation of the Houfe of Commons. That intervention which they had fo frequently refufed to exercife for the prefervation of their country, they now exercifed, at the nod of the minifter, for her deftruction. At a time when the people were juftly complaining of the deftructive influence of the Crown, in a moment when the Houfe of Commons had folemnly refolved that this influence fhould be diminifhed, they *ftood in the gap*, they proved the ready inftruments of the vindictive fpirit of the minifter, and executed the implacable vengeance he had denounced againft the people.

If this country can poffibly efcape the prefent crifis; if ever fhe can hope to reftore her conftitution to her former fpirit and energy, it will be recorded among her annals, with all the becoming pride of national integrity and honour, that a majority of the hereditary peers of England preferved themfelves pure from fo foul a reproach. Scotch peers, and ambitious prelates, penfioners and Lords of the bed-chamber, joined to the members of adminiftration, and Lords in office, alone compofed the degenerate number that rejected the bill.

Mr. Crewe's Bill for preventing Revenue Officers from voting at Elections.

This bill had its fource in the very fpirit of the conftitution. It was introduced on
this

this obvious principle, That to prevent dependance within doors, the speediest method was to secure it without. If the *electors* are corrupted, we can have but little hopes of integrity from the *elected*. Both implicitly obey the mandate of the minister. The one nominates, the other vote in the same spirit.

That the revenue officers can scarce be said to have a franchise; that they can scarce be said to have a vote of their own; that they can in no instance support the candidate their conscience approves, without running the risk of losing their places, it is a fact too notorious to stand in need of proof. Who does not know that the members of the Cinque Ports, and of most of the boroughs on the sea-coast are the representatives of the minister and not of the people? The only possible remedy that could be applied to this evil, was to exclude those creatures of the minister from the right of voting. It was insinuated, that this was a violation of the franchises of the people. But this objection had been obviated by the respectable gentleman who introduced the bill. His only design was to have it established as a rule, that while men possessed offices so immediately under the controul of the minister, their right of voting for members to serve in Parliament should be suspended. If an act for that purpose should pass, there could not be a shadow of hardship to any individual. Every man would know on what ground he was to stand, and would have the option either

M of

of not accepting the office, or of agreeing that his right of voting fhould be fufpended while he held it.

But it was not to be fuppofed, that this ftrong fortrefs of Court influence would be fuffered to be levelled to the ground. The minifter flew to its affiftance with all his force, and the bill was loft at the fecond reading, by a majority of twenty-fix. The very vote that threw it out, was the cleareft proof of the exiftence of the evil it was meant to remove. The reprefentatives of excifemen and cuftom-houfe officers decided the queftion.

Mr. Dunning's Motions upon the Petitions.

Thefe meafures, which the independent gentlemen exerted all their powers to prefs upon the Houfe, though they were bottomed on the prayers of the people, and tended effectually to redrefs their grievances, were not introduced, in confequence of any immediate motion, towards taking the petitions into confideration. This ftep was deferred till the 6th of April. The tranfactions of that day, when compared with the fubfequent conduct of the commons, have fixed a ftain on their journals which no time can efface.

Nothing could be more judicious than the manner in which Mr. Dunning opened this important bufinefs. The people had petitioned

tioned their reprefentatives in a peaceable
and conftitutional manner. It was the undoubted duty of thefe reprefenfatives, to liften
to what thofe who had fent them into parliament had fo ftated, to enquire into the
facts alledged by them in their petitions, and
if they were found to be true, to grant them
immediate and effectual relief. The firft
ftep therefore to be taken, was to appeal to
the Houfe upon the truth of the firft great
allegation of the people. That once determined it would be eafy to proceed to a confideration of the points on which they required relief.

With this view, Mr. Dunning moved,
" that it was the opinion of the Houfe, that
" the influence of the crown had encreafed,
" was encreafing, and ought to be dimi-
" nifhed."

This motion tied the Houfe down at once
to an explicit unequivocal decifion. It was
a refolution of fact, and required no argument. The notoriety of the univerfal pre-
valency of fuch influence, the allegation of
one hundred thoufand freeholders, an allegation exceedingly fimple in itfelf, and which
it was not likely the petitioners would have
made, but upon thorough conviction, the
confcience and feelings of every individual in
the Houfe, were the chief arguments of which
the fuccefs of the motion was made to reft.

The only objection made to it by minifters, befides denying the fact, was, that it was
an abftract propofition, and that fuch pro-

pofitions

positions were never voted by Parliament. This assertion was proved to be false, and an instance to the contrary was given, from the reign of King William, an instance of a question that was voted though *immediately* abstract, which this motion by no means was. This was found to be expressly stated in the petitions, and Mr. Dunning had taken care to obviate the objection, by declaring that the question was designed to be the ground of other resolutions.

While the minister himself appeared distracted, and evidently undecided about the mode of getting rid of the question, the Lord Advocate of Scotland boldly proposed to throw the business out at once, and by moving that the chairman of the committee leave the chair, to give an early decided negative to the prayers of the petitions.

This threw the House into a ferment. Such contemptuous treatment of the people, it was affirmed, could only have originated from one, whose political principles, as far as he has declared them in Parliament, are as foreign to the spirit of the English Constitution, as his accents are barbarous to an English ear.

The minister served to encrease the disorder. While the debate was confined to the motion before the House, he had observed a sullen sulky silence. But, as soon as Mr. Pit, in a torrent of eloquence, charged him with the calamities entailed upon

his

his country ; when he inflanced his continuance in office, as the moft indubitable proof
that could be given, of the enormous influence of the Crown, and fupported this affertion, by a glowing enumeration of all the
tranfactions of his inglorious adminiftration,
his fullenefs gave way to violence and refent-
ment. The juftnefs of the reproaches, and
the confcioufnefs of his guilt, roufed him out
of his ufual phlegmatic infenfibility, and he
burft out into fuch terms of illiberal invective, that an univerfal cry feemed to break
from every part of the Houfe, demanding
that his words might be taken down,

This alarming difcovery, of fo general a
change in the fenfe of the Houfe, feemed to
terrify him. He directed the Lord Advocate
to withdraw his motion. But what this gentleman could not effect by force, he endeavoured to accomplifh by ftratagem. He
moved an amendment, and put it as the main
queftion, that " *it is neceffary now to declare,*
" that the influence of the Crown had en-
" creafed, is encreafing, and ought to be di-
" minifhed."

He afterwards confeffed, that this defign,
in moving this amendment, was to induce
the Houfe to reject the whole propofition.
He was in hopes that the danger, which
would threaten the minifter, if the period of
this increafed influence fhould be fixed to the
time of his adminiftration, as it muft be, by
admitting *the neceffity* of making fuch a declaration

ration *now*, his friends would unite in the defence of their patron, and reject a motion, which from being general, was now become perfonally directed againft the minifter. But he was deceived in his hopes. The gentlemen in the oppofition readily admitted an amendment, that fo forcibly ftrengthened their original propofition, that juftified fo fully the application of the people to their reprefentatives, from the neceffity of the cafe, and that fo clearly fubftantiated their allegations. The queftion was put with its amendment, and was carried by a majority of eighteen.

The principal allegation of the petitions being thus acknowledged, and admitted to be juft, Mr. Dunning proceeded to eftablifh another fundemental propofition. He moved, that it is the opinion of the committee, that it is competent to the Houfe of Commons to examine into, and to correct abufes in the expenditure of the civil-lift revenues, as well as in every other branch of the public revenue, whenever it fhall feem expedient to the wifdom of this Houfe fo to do.

This propofition, the cleareft and moft indifputable that ever was drawn from the conftitution, minifters endeavoured to negative. In the feveral debates on the claufes of Mr. Burke's bill, they had, fome more, fome lefs covertly, laboured to eftablifh a contrary doctrine. They made repeated efforts to have it received as a maxim, that the King had an exclufive right to the monies fettled on him by Parliament; that he had

the

the fame title to his civil lift, which any private gentleman had to his eftate, that it was
as much his own, and that his purfe was too
facred for the other parts of the Legiflature
to controul.

If fuch a doctrine were once eftablifhed,
there would be an end to the conftitution.
For what would be the neceffary confequences of it ? The King might convert his
revenue to what purpofes he fhould think
proper; he might employ it to the deftruction of the ftate, and the fubverfion of the
conftitution. Whatever abufes he might
make of it, Parliament were to be mute
fpectators, and not make a fingle effort to
prevent the mifchief.

If under the reftraint of a parliamentary
power to infpect it, the abufes which were
acknowledged to have fprung from its application were fo extenfive, where would the
mifchief end if this power was to be given
up, and the Houfe of Commons to increafe
the civil revenues in proportion as they had
done of late years, merely on the requifition
of the minifter, without examination or account ? But the fupporters of that dangerous
doctrine were forced to give it up, when it
was thus explicitly put upon iffue. Mr.
Dunning's propofition was admitted without
a divifion.

This refolution was followed by a motion
of Mr. Pitt's, " That it is the duty of the
" Houfe to provide, as far as may be, an
" immediate

" immediate and effectual redrefs of the
" abufes complained of in the petitions, pre-
" fented to the Houfe from the different
" counties, cities and towns, in the kingdom."

This queftion paffed unanimoufly, and the
feveral refolutions having been immediately
reported, the committee broke up and ad-
journed to the 10th.

The proceedings of that day were equally
favorable to the wifhes and expectations of
the people with thofe of the 6th. A motion of Mr. Dunning's for " fecuring the
" independency of parliament, and obviat-
" ing any fufpicion of its purity, by laying
" exact accounts before the Houfe within
" feven days after the firft day of every fef-
" fion, of fuch fum or fums of money as
" have been paid in the courfe of the pre-
" ceding year to Members of Parliament out
" of the civil lift, or any other part of the
" public revenue, to them, to their ufe, or in
" truft for them, or on any other account,
" fpecifying when or on what account fuch
" money was paid," paffed with merely fome
obfervations on the part of the minifter.

His fecond motion, of the fame tendency,
for exc'uding certain placemen, whofe offices
fubjected them to the mandate of the minifter,
from holding feats in Parliament, was, after
a ftrong conteft, carried for the people, on a
divifion of 215 to 213.

This appearance of repentant virtue in
the Commons was received by the people
with all the extravagance of unexpected joy,
and

and the effusions of mutual congratulation.
They received the vote of the 6th as a vote
of atonement from their reprefentatives, and
gave a generous and implicit credit to the affurances they received of obtaining immediate redrefs for the grievances, of which it
was acknowledged they had complained with
juftice. With the moft unfufpecting confidence the counties affumed a milder tone.
They withheld their affociations. They a-
dopted lefs refolute meafures, in the certain
hopes of procuring redrefs from thofe, whom
they were happy to confider once more as
the faithful guardians of their freedom and
poffeffions.

And furely they had the ftrongeft reafons to
flatter themfelves that they fhould be fpeedily
delivered from the deftructive fyftem, and ruinous councils of a fet of men, to whom they
juftly afcribed all their fufferings. For how did
the two hundred thirty-three of their reprefentatives, who voted in the majority of the 6th of
April, ftand pledged to them as gentlemen and
Members of Parliament? They had acknowledged that *now*, under the actual direction
and immediate aufpices of thofe men, the
corrupt influence of the Crown had encreafed
to fo alarming a degree, as to require an immediate and effectual check. With what face
then could they ever after fupport the minifter, who under the preffure of that vote
ftood condemned of having fquandered the
public treafures, and plundered the people in

N   acquiring

acquiring and diffusing that influence? Was there upon record an inftance of fo flagitious a charge having been brought home to any adminiftration, of fo ignominious a fentence having paffed upon any minifter in all the annals of our hiftory? And could the men who confirmed that charge and pronounced that fentence againft his adminiftration, be the perfons to fupport him in office?

They affected to prove their zeal in the fervice of their conftituents, and to recom‑ mend themfelves to their future favor and fupport, by complying with the prayer of their petitions; and could they have the face to fupport the minifter, who in every ftage of that bufinefs, had withftood thofe petitions with all his weight and influence? who, when the fatal effects of his adminiftration firft compelled the freeholders of England to attempt this only expedient *they then had* to fave themfelves and their country from utter ruin, left nothing untried to ftifle them in their birth, and to procure applications of a direct contrary tendency? who branded them with the opprobrious ftigma of fedition, as the offspring of faction, and the laft defperate effort of a contemptible party to force them‑ felves into office? who, fince their introduc‑ tion into the Houfe, had exerted all his pow‑ ‑ers in withftanding every attempt to procure the object of their prayer, and in endeavour‑ ‑ing to defeat every motion grounded on their complaints? and who required no other teft

of

of the fidelity and attachment of his mercenaries, than to go through with him in thofe
infulting proofs of his enmity to the people.

But while the diftant counties indulged
thofe flattering hopes on fuch probable and
obvious grounds, thofe who were nearer the
fcene of action foon began to conceive other
thoughts. The very day after he had been
branded with this ignominious fentence he
had the infolence to appear again before the
Houfe of Commons as the confidential fervant
of his Majefty, and the firft minifter of this
country. His adherents, far from being de-
jected or depreffed, affumed all the haughti-
nefs of a triumph, and boaftingly foretold to
the friends of the people, that their majority
fhould prove a rope of fand.

This unprecedented contempt of the authority of Parliament, and the fubfequent ac-
complifhment of this prediction, have induced many people to fuppofe, that the whole
bufinefs of the 6th was a preconcerted meafure between the minifter and his creatures.

It was a facrifice he permitted them to
make to *the frantic virtue* of their conftituents. Inftead of injuring, it would ferve his
own caufe. By voting that the Crown had
acquired a corrupt influence, while adminiftration was exerting all its powers to prevent
fuch a vote from paffing, they would give
the moft plaufible proof of the falfity of the
accufation. Could fuch an extenfive and
dangerous influence as was complained of,
be confiftent with an oppofition to govern-

ment

ment in fo effential and delicate a point? Their conftituents could not poffibly expect a ftronger proof of their integrity and independence, and muft, on every future occafion, give them credit for voting according to their judgement and confcience.

True they had voted befides, that it was the duty of the Houfe to give the petitioners fome immediate and effectual relief. But this was an abftract queftion that led to nothing. By no conftruction could it be held as binding to any one precife, determined point. Though they had agreed to the propofition, yet they were ftill free to oppofe any mode of reformation that might be propofed by its abettors. This meafure might not pleafe them; that meafure might not come up to their ideas; they might withhold in the detail what they had promifed in the grofs.

Several obfervations that fell from the fpeakers on that fide during the fubfequent debates, tended very ftrongly to confirm thofe fufpicions. The conduct of the trimming members was a ftill ftronger confirmation. This expedient was the exact outline of their proceedings. They rejected every propofition that was offered, with a view of relieving the people to whatever objects it tended, or however framed, but never once propofed a fingle meafure of their own that might acquit the engagement under which they ftood pledged to their conftituents.

If

If this be a true ftatement of the cafe, the fenate of Rome, in her moft degenerate days, when tyrants, who were a reproach to humanity, had reduced that once glorious affembly to the vileft and moft contemptible depth of fervility, never ftooped to fo foul a difgrace. Among all the indignities to which they fubmitted, they never confented to confefs their own infamy by an authentic vote, and to infcribe that confeffion on their records with all the formalities of their legiflative proceedings.

Others, indeed, upon better information afferted, that the loud clamours of the people, and the fears of an approaching election, had fpread a real alarm among the members who did not owe their feats to the immediate gift of the treafury. Thefe felt a momentary terror, and having once deferted from their colors, might, from the apprehenfion of a change of mafters, have perfevered in their defection, had not the minifters made fuch good ufe of the recefs that was occafioned by the illnefs of the Speaker. This event took place while the committee for taking the petitions of the people into confideration were fitting. One of the moft refpectable members in the Houfe, in a debate on the 18th of May, charged the minifter with having employed that period in corrupting the members. To this alone he was indebted for the majority he had regained. If the charge was falfe, he was called upon by another member,

ber, equally refpectable, to apply to the Houfe to have the words taken down, and to bring the fact to difcuffion. But, added this gentleman, " he dare not. He knows the " charge to be too juftly founded. If he " calls for proof, it can be fubftantiated in " his very teeth."

However the people may be difpofed to determine on the caufe of the apoftacy, certain it is, that it appeared in the moft fhamelefs violation of all fhame and decency, immediately on the meeting after this adjournment. The public, by this time, was prepared for the change. The minifter could not contain his triumph on the fuccefs of his negociations with the apoftate members. His adherents took care to publifh abroad the certainty they were in, that on the firft fitting of the committee for the petitions, the oppofition would prove to be what it was foretold it fhould prove a rope of fand. Under thefe impreffions the fupporters of the petitioners went down to the Houfe on the 24th of April. They found their worft fears verified. A motion of Mr. Dunning's for giving fome affurance to the people, that Parliament fhould not be diffolved or prorogued until proper meafures fhould be taken by the Houfe to diminifh the influence, and to correct the other evils of which the petitions complained, and, as the Houfe had acknowledged, with juftice, was rejected by a majority of fifty one.

The

The divifion on this motion completed the triumph of the minifter, and determined at once the fate of the petitions. They were from that moment left at the mercy of an adminiftration hoftile in every point to the prayers of the people, with power to defeat every attempt of reformation by prorogation or diffolution. This power, as was then fore-feen and foretold, they have not failed to exert in the moft arbitrary and contemptuous manner. They firft prorogued and then diffolved the parliament without a fingle ftep having been taken to fulfill the folemn engagement the Houfe had entered into with their confti-tuents.

After that day, the only notice that was taken of the petitions, was to add infult to injury. The minifter feemed to take a pride in aggravating the public fufferings by a mockery of words. He affected to exprefs the utmoft difference to the demands of the people, and the greateft willingnefs to re-drefs their grievances, while he defeated every attempt of the kind on the part of oppofition, without ever fubftituting a fingle expedient of his own.

After that day he lorded in the houfe with his ufual majorities. After that day he pur-fued the great objects of his fyftem without fear or reftraint. The fenfe of duty, the pride of confiftency, the call of honour, the upraidings of confcience, the remembrance of the faith they had folemnly pledged to
their

their conftituents and to each other, were all facrificed to his power by the apoftates from the majority of the 6th of April. They fupported him in his daring encroachment on a privilege, of which the conftitution has been at all times moft tender, and watchful. They authorifed the King's troops to remain in a borough town during the time of election for members of Parliament, and eftablifhed a precedent that will not fail to be improved in the bleffed hands that propofed it. They countenanced the dangerous innovations he introduced into the fyftem of army promotions, and fanctified the abufes by which the navy has been brought to its prefent difgraceful condition. They voted blindly and indifcriminately the enormous fums he demanded for the fervices of the prefent year, far beyond the moft boundlefs profufion of all former periods, and enabled him to reject every application for accounts of the manner in which this plunder on the public fhould be employed. They joined with him in all his fallacious fchemes of raifing new and oppreffive taxes * on the people, in open violation

---

* The annals of mankind cannot exhibit fuch a fcene of minifterial impofition, and political feduction as the prefent firft Lord of the Treafury has practifed by his fyftem of financing, fince the commencement of the American war. A decreafe of taxes, and a diminution of the public burdens was the oftenfible pretext for entering on that accurfed meafure. Thefe were the motives that firft induced the country gentlemen to concur in the hoftile refolutions

that

lation and contempt of their petitions. In
every meafure he propofed they carried their
complaifance beyond even their own former
fervility

that had been formed in the cabinet againft the devoted
Colonifts.

Thefe Colonifts, they were told, had been called upon
to bear a proportinate Share of the heavy incumbrances,
which, chiefly on their own account, had been brought
upon the nation during the laft war. A few ungovernable
fpirits at Bofton had oppofed this claim; but a little ftrenu-
ous exertion, and the very found of hoftile preparations
on our fide would fhortly break this turbulent temper;
and the right of taxation would be admitted in fuch an
extent as to eftablifh a fund of productive lafting revenue.

The miferies that followed thefe fallacious promifes need
no enumeration.—But mark the conduct of our minifter
of finance, as the ruinous circle of, the war enlarged
itfelf.

In the firft two years, one of which was a year of
declared hoftilities, not a fhilling did he borrow. A
veil dark and impenetrable as that he threw over the difpofitions and real fentiments of the Americans, was drawn
over the expenditure, that it might not meet the eye of
the public. By his management of the finking fund, by
difpofing of it without the confent or authority of Parliament, by anticipating its produce; by the credit of the
Bank, and by various fhifts and expedients in the mar-
ket of the unfunded debts, he contrived to let the laft
feffion of 1776 come nigh to a clofe before he applied to
Parliament for the loan of two millions. To pay the
intereft, fome trifling particulars were taxed, that affected
a very fmall part of the people.

The next year, farther claims, and a new loan, But
the people muft be kept in the dark. A tax on fervants
and auctioneers, would not bear very hard on the mafs
of the public.

Another year; and again the fame game. A tax upon
houfes, inconfiderable in itfelf, would only be felt by the
opulent.

O   A

fervility, and seemed anxious to make him ample attonement for the momentary virtue into which they were betrayed. They sunk even below the infamy with which they began their exiftance, and like hardened and defperate finners, encreafed in profligacy as their diffolution approached. In fhort I can venture to affert, and pofterity, at leaft, will confirm the affertion, they have added to the annals of our Parliament, a feries of the moft difgracing, profligate, deftructive proceedings that ever ftained the journals of the Commons.

On the 8th of June, the feffions was concluded by a fpeech from the throne; and on the ift of September, the Parliament was diffolved. Whether this be a bleffing or not, muft remain with the freeholders to deter-

A fourth year came, with ftill encreafing expences; but the rich, and thofe who could indulge themfelves in fuperfluous eafe, were alone to fuffer. Poft chaifes, and poft horfes were taxed.—In fhort a debt of upwards of twenty millions, drawing after it an intereft of more than a million *per annum*, was artfully, and by ftealth *flipped*, if I may be allowed the expreffion, on the public; and when the upfhot of the means propofed to raife the intereft came to be examined, we found that the taxes were fo delufive and unproductive, that they did not amount to one half of what they were taken for—Thus the taxes that have been this year laid on fome of the immediate neceffaries of life are but the beginning of our miferies.—The people already complain of infufferable burdens, but what will it be when they find themfelves obliged, not only to bear the preffure of new loans and encreafing expences, but to provide likewife for the deficiencies of years paft which they were falfely told, had been born exclufively by the fuperiour claffes.

mine.

mine. By the prefent choice of the reprefentatives, that queſtion, and others of equal
importance, muſt be decided. A few weeks
will prove how far the only hopes we had
left of efcaping the final ruin with which our
conſtitution and ſtate are threatened by a perfeverance in the prefent ſyſtem, are founded,
or if the record of degeneracy muſt equally
ſtigmatize the Parliament and people of
England.

FINIS.

www.ingramcontent.com/pod-product-compliance
Lightning Source LLC
Chambersburg PA
CBHW032200010726
47493CB00008BA/2772